IMPLEMEN
EVIDENCE-BASED RESEARCH
A How-To Guide for Police Organizations

Laura Huey, Renée J. Mitchell,
Hina Kalyal and Roger Pegram

First published in Great Britain in 2021 by

Policy Press, an imprint of Bristol University Press
University of Bristol
1-9 Old Park Hill
Bristol
BS2 8BB
UK
t: +44 (0)117 954 5940
e: bup-info@bristol.ac.uk

Details of international sales and distribution partners are available at
policy.bristoluniversitypress.co.uk

British Library Cataloguing in Publication Data
A catalogue record for this book is available from the British Library.

ISBN 978-1-4473-5359-1 paperback
ISBN 978-1-4473-5360-7 ePub
ISBN 978-1-4473-5362-1 ePdf

Cover design: Andrew Corbett
Front cover image: iStock-1098410490

Bristol University Press and Policy Press use environmentally
responsible print partners

Printed in Great Britain by CMP, Poole

Contents

List of tables and figures

Tables

Figures

Acknowledgments

The authors would like to thank Chief Andrew Fletcher, Deputy Chief Colin Watson, Assistant Chief Constable Chris Noble, Assistant Chief Constable Chris Sykes, Commander Rachel Tolber, Captain Jason Potts, and Staff-Sergeant Natalie Hiltz for their contributions.

This book would not have been possible without funding through the Social Sciences and Humanities Research Council of Canada Partnership Development Grant.

Introduction

> Okay, we're sold. But now what? (Question asked
> by a police chief)

About 20 years ago, Lawrence Sherman (1998) wrote an article
for the National Police Foundation in the USA that set out two
important challenges:

- For police agencies: to participate in the creation and use of
  high-quality research to guide the development of evidence-
  based policy, programs and practices.
- For researchers: to craft scientific work that can be readily
  understood and used by police services.

The rationale? To learn from what the combination of science
and police expertise can tell us 'works' (and what doesn't) in
relation to various aspects of public policing, from reducing
burglaries to deterring gun violence.

Since Sherman's famous challenge, we've seen the global
growth of evidence-based policing (EBP) into a movement
of sorts that has spawned four Societies of Evidence-Based
Policing (in the UK, Canada, the USA, and Australia and New
Zealand) numbering thousands of members. There are annual
conferences, training seminars, books, articles, and various tools
and resources to help the budding EBP practitioner. But so far,
despite various attempts at laying out some general ideas and
principles (see Martin, 2018), what no one has been willing
to tackle is the dreaded question posed to us after nearly every
presentation or training session we've led: 'How do you actually
do this stuff?'

In this book, we tackle this question in a practical, nuts and
bolts sort of way, offering ideas and suggestions drawn from
both our own research into embedding EBP and from the

broader research literature. To be clear: this is not your standard criminology book — we don't breathlessly recite all of the latest and greatest findings from criminological research (although there will be plenty of that too). Instead, our focus is on how individuals and organizations can become more evidence-based.

To become more evidence-based requires some understanding of change and how individuals and organizations can become change agents, and to that end, we draw on knowledge from a diverse array of fields that can help illuminate different possibilities for generating change. These include studies in management, military leadership, medicine, policy-making, health sciences, and policing research. If you like to be exposed to different ways of thinking, you're in luck.

What is this evidence-based policing of which you speak?

If you're reading a book on how to implement EBP, we presume you have some familiarity with the philosophy. That said, it never hurts to have a short refresher.

Evidence-based policing is an approach that focuses equal attention on the methods used to conduct research as on its subsequent translation and use. Perhaps the single best definition of EBP we have seen comes from the UK College of Policing (2018):

> Evidence-based policing is an approach in which police officers and staff work with academics and other partners to create, review, and use the best available evidence to inform and challenge policing policies, practices, and decisions.

The reason we like this definition is that it places the emphasis on police practitioners and agencies to adopt, create, and use research evidence, with academics and others playing supportive roles. This view of EBP stands in stark contrast to more traditional research partnerships, in which academics are often seen as not only dictating the research agenda, but also often producing work of little practical value (Bradley and Nixon, 2009).

EBP is a challenge to police to examine their programs, policies, and practices to ensure they are not only meeting desired outcomes, but doing so without producing any unintended negative consequences (a 'backfire effect'). As Sherman (2013) has observed, police practices have historically tended to result more from experience than from conscious design and evaluation. Thus, 'most police practices, despite their enormous cost, are still untested' (Sherman, 2013: 384). For the EBP practitioner, '[EBP] is a process that begins with a willingness to enter a workplace and pose what can often be a challenging question: "Why do we do that?"' (Murray, 2018: 215).

Chief Andrew Fletcher,
South Simcoe Police
Service, Ontario, Canada

There is much talk about an 'evidence-based approach' in policing, but for many front-line cops, and just as many police leaders, what does that mean and why is it important?

In many ways, it seems like a new label has been put on something that some have been doing for years. We never arrest anyone or act without gathering all of the 'evidence'. At the center of our very own use of force model are the words 'assess – plan – act', and we encourage our people to follow that continuum when determining the appropriate action to take in any situation. So why is that any different when determining a strategic approach to our business? When dealing with personnel issues, I have always encouraged people to not react to what they are told, but to gather all of the evidence before making a decision. There are two sides to every story, whether dealing with our people or working through a complex investigation. It is important to slow things down, gather all of the evidence, and then address the situation and put processes or policies in place to ensure the behaviour or situation does not re-occur.

So let's not over-complicate things by using fancy buzz words or formal definitions. Before taking action on something, whether developing a new program, investigative strategy, or organizational practice, take the time to gather all of the evidence and look at what research exists that can help inform your decision or action.

One way to break down EBP is to think about it in terms of the 'triple-T': targeting, testing, and tracking (Sherman, 2013). *Targeting* refers to the identification of a high priority problem, whether it be a place, crime pattern, type of offense, and so on (Sherman and Murray, 2015). Once identified, police responses should be *tested* through systematic analysis aimed at determining whether responses meet desired objectives (Sherman, 2015). Once implemented, practices should be *tracked* and the resulting data used to generate assessments as to the delivery and effects of changes within the institution and in the larger community (Sherman, 2015). What marks EBP as different from conventional policing research is that post-study implementation and tracking are key factors to building a solid knowledge base of research that can potentially be transferred and adapted to other sites (Neyroud, 2015). EBP is thus about:

- Testing experience-based intuitions or ideas with the best methods.
- Using the evidence to target police effort at the most effective strategies and tactics by focusing on places, victims, and offenders.
- Building an evidence base on how best to implement and how best to adapt and translate tested evidence from one context to another (Neyroud, 2015).

In short, there are five key ideas behind EBP (Telep and Lum, 2014; Sherman, 2015):

- Scientific research has a role to play in developing effective and efficient policing programs.
- Research produced must meet standards of methodological rigor *and* be useful to policing.

- Results should be easily translatable into everyday police practice and policy.
- Research should be the outcome of a blending of police experience with academic research skills.
- Policing issues should be addressed through careful targeting, testing, and tracking of implemented solutions.

To figure out how well your agency is doing in terms of these key ideas, a good starting point might be to consider the following questions, which we have borrowed from Peter Martin (2018).

General questions

- Does your agency use existing research?
- Does your agency invest in the creation of new research?
- Are your major police practices or strategies informed by research?

Program- or practice-specific questions

- Is the police practice informed by research?
- Does an evidence base exist for the practice?
- Is the research translatable (or implementable)?
- Is there a need to change or modify the existing research to make it implementable?

What types of activities fall under evidence-based policing?

There is also a lot more to becoming evidence-based from an organizational standpoint beyond running program evaluations. At its best, it's a holistic approach to decision-making that draws on scientific research to think through how best to deal with operational, administrative, social, and other issues within policing or faced by police officers. This doesn't mean, however, that every agency will become 100 percent evidence-based all of the time. Further, this philosophy, when practiced, will necessarily differ for reasons we discuss below.

Given the emphasis placed on finding out 'what works' in policing, not surprisingly a lot of attention has been paid to the role of evaluation research within EBP, particularly the use of randomized controlled trials (RCTs) to determine if programs are producing their intended effects. While evaluating programs is an important component of EBP work, EBP can also include a range of other types of research and research-related activities. Table 0.1 below provides a brief look at some other research possibilities.

Here are just a few of the types of research–related activities that can be adopted by individuals and organizations:

- Incorporating crime analysis and/or discussion of relevant research within operational and management meetings (Lum and Koper, 2017).
- Providing evidence-based training that draws on the relevant scientific research (Sherman, 2015).
- Using crime analysis to target crime hotspots (Lum and Koper, 2017).
- Establishing an organizational research committee or working group (Martin, 2018).
- Conducting surveys of officers to evaluate crime reduction strategies (Santos, 2017).

Table 0.1: General categories of research

Research type	Purpose	Methods	Examples of study
Exploratory	To develop new ideas and insights into a topic of which little is known	Qualitative/ quantitative	Interviews; focus groups; content analysis; ethnography
Descriptive	To describe a phenomenon or characteristics of a group of people	Qualitative/ quantitative	Surveys; interviews; focus groups; case studies; observational studies; ethnography
Causal or confirmatory	To assess if something works by showing that one (program A) causes the other (outcome B)	Quantitative	RCTs; quasi-experimental designs; pre-/post-test designs

Source: Authors' own

- Embedding a PhD-level researcher within a police organization to conduct research, review policies, and programs and/or assist with training (Braga and Davis, 2014; Sherman, 2015).
- Partnering with researchers and community members to carry out research (Lum and Koper, 2017).
- Identifying an EBP ambassador to promote EBP within an agency (Martin, 2018).
- Creating a research or EBP unit (Sherman, 2015).
- Supporting police officers and civilian analysts in applied degree programs (Sherman, 2015).

The above is, of course, not meant to be an exhaustive list. However, it does provide a useful starting point for thinking about the diverse array of opportunities available for engaging in EBP. We will have a lot more to say about these and other methods for engaging in evidence-based practices in the chapters to follow. However, before we conclude this section, we want to note one additional thing: many police organizations already use evidence-based practices to some degree, including, perhaps, some of those listed above. The issue then becomes one of commitment, as in, does EBP within that agency entail a 'regular, institutionalized and consistent use of research, analysis and science to inform a broad range of activities' (Lum and Koper, 2017: 134)? If not, some of the ideas we describe in later chapters, and have tested in the field, may be of some help.

There is no master plan

We need to be clear on one thing: while there is a wealth of great ideas available to practitioners and agencies seeking to become more evidence-based, there is, alas, no 'master plan', no 'one true way', and no 'out of the box solutions' for how to get there. The reality is that what works for one individual or agency may not work for another because of a host of contingent factors, including resources, funding, local culture, local politics, and geographical and historical contexts, just to name a few. This hasn't, in the past, however, stopped police services from engaging in something called 'naive policy transfer' or 'naive emulation' – the practice of implementing a policy, program, or practice solely because it was successful elsewhere, and often without regard for whether the situations were close enough to ensure success in the new location (Stenson and Edwards, 2001). We do not advocate for that here. Instead, we suggest a much more radical approach: figuring out what potential solutions will work for a given agency based on needs and resources (*targeting*), implementing and evaluating each strategy or solution against desired outcomes (*testing*), and then ensuring they continue to work over time, adjusting when needed or axing those that don't (*tracking*). In other words, we advocate for an experimental process in which progress occurs incrementally, rather than as a result of a GrandVision™.

To illustrate what we mean, we offer two examples below of very different processes two agencies took towards attempting to embed EBP (see Table 0.2). For some context, we note both agencies are medium-sized, municipal Canadian police services, albeit operating in different provinces. Both agencies also have crime analytics departments, but one has a complement of 600 sworn officers and the other has approximately 200 sworn members. The other thing both share is each is continuing to incrementally develop their programs.

This flexible approach to implementing EBP might be intimidating to some. However, we want to point out that in adopting such a position, you would be in excellent company. Let's take the case of the consumer products giant, Apple. When Steve Jobs returned to Apple in 1997, it was in a state of financial crisis, near collapse. Before his death in 2011, he turned it into a powerhouse. How? Jobs built Apple products incrementally and by synthesizing strands of ideas in new ways, including sometimes combining ideas that didn't work, or that didn't work well in one context but worked brilliantly in another. Take the Apple iTunes store as an example. The origins of iTunes came from the realization that programmers from his less successful venture, NeXT, had software that could easily provide downloadable mp3 files through a file-sharing service that would allow consumers to pay for the products they wanted (Schlender and Tetzeli, 2015). Once he built iTunes, he negotiated for content with the big music companies, creating what has been described as a cultural 'revolution' (Knopper, 2013). Next step:

Table 0.2: Different adoption styles

Step	Agency A (600 members)	Agency B (200 members)
1	Embedded a criminologist through a research fellow position	EBP training seminar
2	Ran several studies with the research fellow and her students	Set up an EBP working group
3	Senior member of command staff enrolled in the Cambridge University MSt in Police Leadership (EBP program)	Participated in an EBP assessment survey to set a baseline for future growth
4	Set up an internal EBP working group	Filed a research grant with a criminologist to conduct a joint EBP study on a topic produced from the working group
5	Held three training seminars for frontline personnel	Held a subsequent seminar
6	Supported a mid-career officer in enrolling for the Cambridge EBP program	Started a research project with outside academic researchers
7	Developed more internal training and research support with courses and projects related to 'critical thinking' and 'problem-solving'	
8	Plans to create an EBP unit	

Source: Authors' own

realizing the engineers at Apple hated the existing mp3 players, he set out to do what Apple arguably does best, build a 'whole widget' by integrating Apple hardware and software to produce the iPod (Isaacson, 2011). It is worth noting that whenever Jobs went for GrandVisions™, he failed (Schlender and Tetzeli, 2015). Along the way, Jobs and Apple tried some things, made some mistakes, and shelved or killed projects that didn't work. This is what we do as EBP practitioners, and it is what we are asking you to consider doing as well.

Does size really matter?

Let's face it: we live in a world in which bigger is all too frequently seen as better. We would argue this is no less the case with police service size, where bigger is often seen to mean more resources, more people, more opportunities, more technology, more programs, and, perhaps most importantly, more funding. But is bigger necessarily a good thing when it comes to the question of trying to effect system-wide change? After all, EBP is a holistic approach to the question of how best to go about the business of policing. It requires a fundamental shift in how agencies – at every level of an organization – make decisions on important questions centered on internal and external efficacy and efficiency.

Whereas other books on implementing organizational change typically focus on core themes, one of the things we have done differently is to organize this book around the interests of potential readers, some of whom may be working within smaller agencies, others in medium-to-large-sized police services. While this may seem to be an unconventional approach, the reality is that when it comes to openness to research and the willingness to implement EBP, size (of police agencies) *really* does matter (see Telep, 2017). Organizational size affects everything from patterns of decision-making, available resources, to possible investments in institutionalizing EBP.

To illustrate, a frequent comment heard from representatives of medium-sized agencies (101–999 sworn members) is that while they have some resources, namely, in the form of crime analysts, these analysts are already steadily employed with keeping track of their agency's patrol and other statistics. Thus, engaging in EBP research is seen to represent an additional burden for which employees may not be ready. Compare this to the situation of a larger agency, such as the New York Police Department (NYPD), which developed the CompStat model (NYPD's crime data program), and it might be easy to see how, comparatively speaking, larger agencies can serve as incubators for new ideas that grow to influence policing as a whole. And yet, both the research literature and our own experiences working with larger agencies reveal that larger services come with their own internal and external issues that can make change difficult. Change within larger police agencies often seems like turning a battleship, as it takes time and effort, particularly when compared to smaller agencies that, due to their size, are often more flexible and therefore more easily adaptable (see Telep, 2017).

In this book we characterize agencies as small, medium, and large by the number of sworn officers they employ (see Table 0.3). The International Association of Chiefs of Police (IACP, USA) designates services as 'small' that employ fewer than 50 police officers, 'mid-sized' as 50–999 and 'large' (or major cities) agencies as 1,000 or more sworn officers. For the most part, we use these numbers to help us and you think through what you need to know in relation to agency size. However, we have made one adjustment. The IACP's classification of mid-sized makes a great deal of sense in the US context, where there are some 18,000 police services, a sizable proportion of which are comprised of fewer than 50 officers. In Canada, the UK and many other countries, there are few services of that size, and these would generally be considered small. So, we break it down as follows:

Table 0.3: Size breakdown

Agency size	Sworn members
Small	1–99
Medium	100–999
Large	1,000+

Source: Authors' own

What comes next?

We have organized the chapters of this book to make it relatively easy for readers to pick and choose among those topics and situations that are the most relevant. For example, some readers will be hoping to better understand how they can employ evidence-based frameworks within their organizations as individual change agents; others might be police leaders looking for tools and strategies to implement EBP within their small, medium, or large organization. That said, we strongly advise you to read each chapter. Many of the ideas we introduce in the chapter on smaller agencies can also be of use to those working within larger organizations.

To help situate the reader, we begin by focusing on change and the question of how to drive it within organizations. The reality is that police services today face tremendous pressure to constantly change and innovate to meet increasing performance expectations and budgetary constraints. Incorporating the use of applied research evidence can greatly enhance the efficiency and effectiveness of these organizations; however, the response towards adoption of EBP is not without its challenges. In *Chapter 1* we explore factors that facilitate or hinder the adoption of such practices by police organizations. To do so, we draw not only on the relevant EBP literature, but also on the literature in organizational change and the diffusion of innovation to identify such factors present in the external and internal organizational environment. In this overview, we also provide practical solutions to help embed and promote EBP in police organizations.

Chapters 2 and 3 are intended to help those who are new to EBP and the world of policing research by providing some much-needed context. We do this in *Chapter 2* by situating EBP in relation to some of the more common policing philosophies and models, namely, problem-oriented policing, community-oriented policing, and intelligence-led policing. Understanding that some of the similarities among models can cause confusion, we highlight key differences, as well as areas of overlap, to show how an EBP framework can be used in ways that help support other approaches.

Our purpose in *Chapter 3* is to provide an overview of research methods, as well as a brief introduction to some of the more common methods for conducting studies found in policing research. You'll be happy to hear our intention is not to overwhelm the reader with jargon and formulas. However, to understand how best to employ the 'triple-T' strategy in a police service, a basic level of knowledge of research concepts, ideas, and principles is required. Some of this knowledge will likely also prove useful for those starting out in accessing existing research and/or with an interest in conducting their own studies.

In *Chapter 4*, we shift our focus to the individual as an EBP advocate. As we note, early adopters of any practice are often vilified, mocked, or at a minimum, ostracized from the group. Introducing a new way of critically examining policy and practice is uncomfortable for most professions, but in policing, where rank and hierarchy stand above all other considerations, attempting to advance a scientific approach to policing on your own can be daunting.

As EBP is still in its relative infancy, we see more of an individualistic approach to introducing EBP in an organization rather than a whole agency approach. Therefore, our focus in Chapter 4 is on the different paths EBP advocates can take in learning about EBP, implementing EBP, and the ramifications of becoming an EBP advocate within their organization. To do so, we provide specific examples of how early advocates were introduced to EBP and what steps they took to learn more about this approach. We also explore the unique approaches these early adopters used to advance EBP practices within their own organizations and, most importantly, we discuss the professional ramifications advocates face as they are often competing against an orthodoxy where gut feelings, intuition, and tradition win out over research-based approaches.

Chapters 5, 6, and 7 provide solutions to the question of how to implement EBP within police organizations of varying sizes, structures, and resources and within different occupational, cultural, and other environments. To do this, we draw not only on the relevant research literature, but also on individual case studies.

Throughout *Chapter 5* we reveal the various ways in which smaller can also be better when it comes to adopting an evidence-based approach to creating and managing organizational policy and practice. Drawing on our own extensive experience with working with smaller agencies (fewer than 100 sworn officers), we identify key strengths that smaller agencies can harness to effect change. To help round out our perspective, we also include vignettes from police officers in smaller services that have themselves adopted EBP within their own organizations.

In *Chapter 6*, we examine issues related to resources and other arguments, to show how mid-sized agencies are often perfectly positioned to adopt evidence-based approaches. Whereas they have greater resources than smaller agencies, they also often lack the complex – indeed, sometimes byzantine – hierarchical structures and routines of larger agencies. Through examining the relevant research literature, our own work implementing

EBP with medium-sized agencies, we discuss both the advantages of the mid-sized agency, as well as the barriers or limitations they may face, when it comes to commissioning, conducting, and using research to inform decision-making. We also offer constructive solutions for minimizing impediments and overcoming structural and other barriers.

In *Chapter 7*, we examine the relative strengths and limitations of embedding EBP within major municipal, regional, provincial, and/or state-level agencies. To illustrate how it can be done, we draw on our experiences of working within one large municipal service that decided to adopt EBP as a departmental philosophy. To help the reader understand what larger agencies can face, we explore this agency's struggles to figure out the best way to implement organizational change – from their various starts and stops, to the decision to re-examine their approach, we walk through the process by which this organization slowly embedded EBP values that led to changes in policies and practices.

Incorporating evidence-based practices into an organization is not a simple endeavour. Cultural change is difficult, no matter the level of willingness. To effectively implement EBP practices, partnerships are often crucial. A partner can serve as an unbiased third party to assist with the implementation of EBP, whether this is simply informing the agency about the state of the research, designing an experiment, or helping to develop evidence-based policies.

In *Chapter 8*, we review and, where necessary, expand on key points made throughout the text. Our focus, however, is on sustainability. In particular, we examine the institutional, structural and resource issues as well as other issues that need to be addressed to embed change within police organizations and create a sustainable culture of learning and inquiry.

To round out this book, *Chapter 9* provides practitioners and other readers with an introduction to many of the resources that are currently available to support EBP as a practice. From websites to virtual conferences and podcasts, there are many educational opportunities to learn more about EBP, tools to practice EBP, and opportunities to interact with others who are similarly trying to learn and/or incorporate evidence-based approaches.

1

Implementing evidence-based policing

The entire premise of evidence-based policing (EBP), with its emphasis on 'what works', should, in theory, be of immense appeal to police services. After all, we have a sizeable body of research that shows how programs and strategies based on sound research can contribute significantly to police effectiveness and efficiency (Lum, 2009). For example, proactive strategies such as CompStat (Computerized Statistics), problem-oriented policing (POP), intelligence-led policing (ILP) (Ratcliffe, 2008), and hotspots policing (Sherman and Weisburd, 1995) have been found to be more effective compared to random and reactive models. Research by Braga and Weisburd (2010) shows that an evidence-based approach was effective in reducing crime when adopted by police services in the USA by helping officers to focus on areas with a greater incidence of crime. And yet, despite such research, uptake of EBP by police organizations has generally been rather slow (Lum et al, 2012). Why is that?

In this chapter, we take an organizational perspective, looking first at factors that affect police receptiveness to EBP, and then later identifying factors that affect resistance. Our goal: to help both police practitioners and their services move beyond various institutional obstacles and stumbling blocks.

Factors affecting receptivity to evidence-based policing practices

Evidence-based practices are expected to help police organizations enhance their knowledge base, effectiveness, and economic efficiency (Bierly et al, 2009). One would assume that given the noted benefits of EBP, there would be abundant research identifying factors that help foster receptivity and reduce resistance to these practices. Surprisingly, such studies are few and far between, and a majority of them do not provide a clear idea about the impact of organizational context on embedding EBP in police organizations. So what is organizational context, and why should we care? Allow us to explain.

Organizational context refers to the factors that make up the external and internal organizational environment. These factors, individually and collectively, can have the capacity to impede or facilitate organizational change. External environments include political, social, economic, or technological factors (Spector, 2011), while the internal organizational environment comprises of institutional resources, organizational structure, culture, and prior experience of change (Reichers et al, 1997). We will first discuss factors in the external organizational environment affecting receptivity to EBP, drawing on the few available studies on the topic (see Figure 1.1).

Figure 1.1: Environmental factors affecting receptivity to EBP

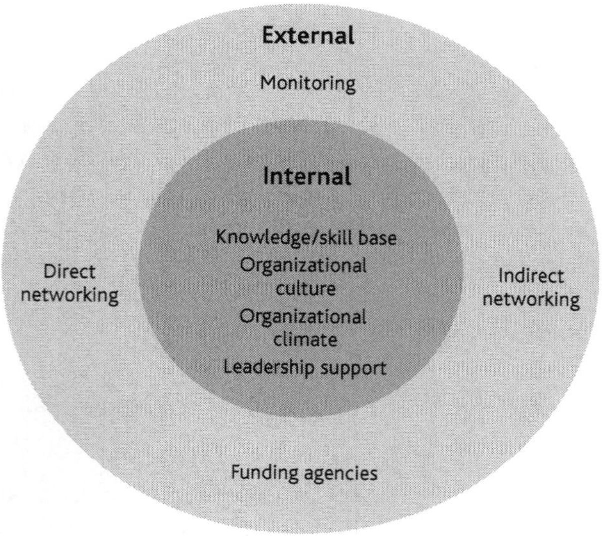

Source: Authors' own

Our search of available research revealed that monitoring and review of police organizations by external stakeholders is one of the key factors driving receptivity to EBP. Police organizations have also been motivated by the growing emphasis on accountability to furnish police boards with scientific measures of performance. Public expectations of better performance, and high expectations of accountability, especially in relation to decision-making, rejects anecdotal reporting and is the impetus behind the adoption of the evidence-based model. EBP enables accurate evaluation of programs and successful measurement of outputs and objectives, which are important in justifying organizational decisions. Against the backdrop of diminishing budgets, police organizations have to prove effective adoption of innovative strategies while making a bid to secure government funding.

Another factor believed to facilitate receptivity to EBP is direct networking with external researchers. Building trust-based collaborative working relations with academics outside the organization can help agencies gain a better perspective regarding EBP adoption and projects based on EBP. Simply put, sometimes police agencies require objective and expert opinion for the improvement of organizational performance. Further, the practical experience of policing combined with the academic expertise of external researchers could develop a better understanding of the EBP philosophy within police organizations. One such example of successful police–researcher collaboration can be found in a study by Kalyal (2019). A police superintendent explained how an unusually high number of homicides in their region made them realize the importance of research. They sought the help of a local academic, who enabled them to target high-risk areas and eventually reduce the number of crimes.

Indirect networking with other agencies and individuals through platforms such as the Societies of Evidence-Based Policing (SEBP) that are operating in the USA, UK, Canada, Australia and New Zealand, are also instrumental in enhancing receptivity to EBP. Police practitioners tend to exhibit greater reliance on information from their professional colleagues and opinion leaders than on sources in academia. Therefore, the establishment of such forums is highly beneficial where academics, practitioners, and experts alike can benefit from the latest developments in their field and contextualize the knowledge to their own settings. Becoming part of the EBP community helps move police organizations closer to a more evidence-based-driven organization. Also, networking through such channels would enable them to learn from other agencies and tailor successful programs to their individual needs while avoiding duplication and wastage of resources.

In terms of inner contextual factors influencing receptivity to EBP, the ability of a police organization to apply externally obtained knowledge to its advantage is an important factor. This ability is enhanced through the diversity of education and skillset in tandem with specialized positions supporting the application and sharing of research within the organization. Openness to new ideas depends on the level of existing skills and knowledge base of the employees, and having a dedicated and diverse group of researchers for exploring and facilitating EBP. Hiring officers with a minimum of undergraduate level degrees as well as full-time researchers and external consultants is also instrumental in EBP adoption. The role of police executives, managers, and supervisors in encouraging evidence-based practices is especially important in this regard. They must be mindful of the evidence while making decisions on how police resources are deployed and whether a program is effective or not.

Another important factor is organizational culture (norms and values). Agencies that are open to change, and willing to engage in calculated risk-taking, are going to be more receptive to EBP. Internally driven changes in step with organizational culture find easier acceptance than changes that are not familiar. It goes back to the whole idea of more proactive, preventive, intervention-based policing tactics, rather than the traditional, reactive calls for service. Police agencies should make efforts to align organizational culture and EBP strategies through consultation with members of the organization to ensure a culture strategy fit for EBP adoption. Leadership should focus on inculcating innovation as a core cultural value and be the stewards and consolidators of change. This can be achieved through new recruits with higher levels of education, who are likely to create a cultural shift towards the use of evidence. Organizational support is also a key factor to bring about a cultural change. Provision of adequate resources and research material across the board with the expectation of making evidence-based decisions would also be helpful in changing the old reactive mindset. Because it takes at least a generation to transform cultural norms, major organizational changes like EBP involve a time-intensive and adaptive process. A gradual shift in police culture is required to embrace research-based practices, as many earlier practices can no longer be justified.

Receptivity to EBP is also influenced by organizational climate, which is linked to organizational culture. Here it would be useful to distinguish between the two concepts. While organizational culture represents the values and norms, the climate of an organization is grounded in the perceptions of employees regarding organizational expectations of employee behaviour. It therefore plays a significant role in creating openness to change. Police organizations are accustomed to emulating agencies that have a demonstrated record of program effectiveness, to avoid wastage of available resources. In terms of EBP adoption, agencies make efforts to observe effective EBP strategies locally and internationally to determine what works and how new ideas and new research findings can be incorporated into organizational practices. Thus the management should focus on the acquiring and application of knowledge while incentivizing receptivity towards EBP among members of the organization. It would appear that specifically targeting change-related behaviour with rewards and incentives could contribute to the development of an organizational climate that is viewed as being receptive towards innovation, thus mobilizing organizational change.

Leadership support is a prominent factor of influence on receptivity towards EBP. The head of a police organization is always instrumental in setting a strategic direction for the agency based on research, ingraining it into the organizational culture. They help in augmenting the capacity for innovation by introducing as well as supporting initiatives that represent organizational change. Support of this nature is viewed as a balancing force by members of the organization, which can neutralize threats to practitioner identities and improve receptivity towards EBP. Top management's level of education and exposure to research is also key to EBP adoption. Police leaders who keep themselves updated on developments in research tend to challenge members of the organization to try new things. Educated leaders have the capacity to mine the environment for innovative ideas and to support the adoption of these ideas by boosting employee capacities and confidence. As adopting new ideas entails developing expertise as well as knowledge to address prospective challenges, highly educated leaders are likely to handle such challenges more skilfully.

Now that we've discussed in detail the factors that affect police receptivity to EBP, it would also be useful to get a sense of those elements present in a police agency's external and internal environment that make them resistant towards EBP.

Factors affecting resistance to evidence-based policing

While EBP might be the future of effective policing, as suggested by Sherman (1998), a lack of enthusiasm has been observed on the part of police organizations towards adopting EBP. Bayley (1994) has pointed out that persuading police practitioners to subscribe to practices based on research is difficult, which is evident in the largely unsuccessful efforts to embed EBP, especially within the North American context. Changes and uncertainty arising out of the implementation of EBP can give rise to police resistance to the approach itself. While it is natural for individuals to resist change due to the accompanying uncertainty, there must be an effort to address these reactions, if new initiatives are to gain traction.

Police organizations tend to follow a reactive approach to policing dominated by procedure, tradition, and culture. This contrasts sharply with the EBP approach that entails major transformations in the management of human and physical resources. As an example, we may turn to Mastrofski and Willis (2010), who point out that the law enforcement agencies do not generally like civilians interfering in their work, whereas an EBP approach, such as problem-oriented policing, may call on the police to solve issues in the community through soliciting civilian input. In a similar manner, other initiatives such as problem-oriented policing as well as intelligence-led law enforcement pose a challenge to the traditional way of policing focusing on calls for service and identifying and analysing problems. In view of the foregoing discussion, we argue that resistance to EBP may arise from a range of contextual factors present in the internal and external organizational environment (see Figure 1.2). Let's discuss the internal organizational factors first.

Lack of communication and training within the organization regarding the need for EBP is one of the major reasons behind the slow adoption of new initiatives. For successful implementation of change initiatives, it is important to create open communication so that members of the organization can identify the link between the innovation and its alignment with organizational goals. In this regard, the hierarchical composition of law enforcement agencies is believed to obstruct effective communication to a great extent, thus making it difficult for members of the organization, especially frontline officers, to take part in the change underway. As a result, EBP becomes a mere

Figure 1.2: Environmental factors affecting resistance

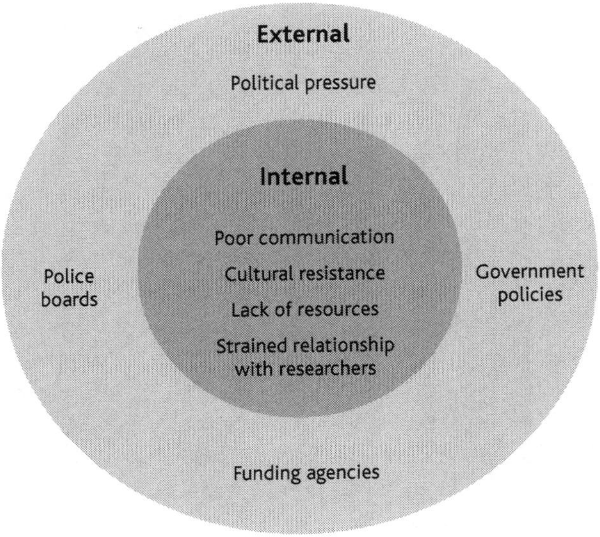

Source: Authors' own

catchphrase instead of a serious initiative. As most communication in police organizations is filtered through departmental channels, it is necessary to share information on EBP via training or organizational communication to prevent ambiguity.

The importance of providing timely feedback on the outcomes of a new initiative cannot be overstated. Tangible results of EBP initiatives must be shared with members of the organization to overcome resistance to EBP, and to make them realize the value of their work. Demonstrating the value of new strategies and how they affect the public also encourages members of the organization to appreciate the evidence-based approach. The lack of adherence to evidence-based practices can also be traced back to a lack of training and guidance on implementing the innovation. The issue is significant enough for Martin and Mazerolle (2016) to contend that police leadership should allocate 10 percent of the organizational discretionary budget towards research as well as training and development, so that EBP can be implemented effectively.

Cultural resistance also affects the police response towards EBP. Edgar Schein (1988) has noted that organizational culture, which can be defined as a matrix of values and norms shared by members of the organization, significantly influences successful change implementation. Resistance to change stems from the organizational culture remaining static, despite the need for it to evolve. Due to the para-militaristic nature found within most police organizations, and the inherent conservatism of policing in general, police organizations tend to be reluctant towards using research to undertake decision-making. One of us, Laura, experienced a version of this first-hand while conducting training with frontline officers in a municipal service. The idea that officers might be willing to share research ideas informally with command staff elicited a grim look on one person's face, who replied more than once, "We have a chain of command!" Cultural resistance to change stems from comfort with the status quo. While concerns with maintaining hierarchy are one consideration, this resistance can also be based on the belief that police know their job best and have always done things a certain way. Such complacency can lead to the failure of any new initiative if not managed correctly.

Sometimes there's also a political aspect associated with resistance, as the public is used to receiving policing services a certain way. Hence the removal or changes in services can often meet with the disapproval of external oversight bodies or by the general public. An excellent example of this is the controversy over the decision by Leicestershire Police in the UK to trial an experiment involving scene of crime officers (SOCOs). Recognizing that the quality and quantity of forensic evidence at an attempted break and enter is likely to be too low to be of value, they ran an experiment in which SOCOs (also known as crime scene investigators or forensic identification officers) were sent to attempted break and enters at houses with even numbers only (along with a constable); houses with odd numbers received a constable only. What the experiment revealed is that there was no additional evidentiary or other value to sending a SOCO to an attempted break and enter. It also revealed that the media and the public, not understanding the study or the importance of this finding, hated the idea.

Risk aversion or fear of failure is another one of the cultural barriers to EBP. While we acknowledge the professional capability of the police to deal with investigations and violent confrontations, there are areas where the police would need help from academia. A challenge with policing culture is that members of police organizations tend not to admit making mistakes or having weaknesses. In such a situation, there is no opportunity to reflect on or learn from errors, whereas evidence-based practices are all about continuous learning.

The human and financial resources of police organizations are also significant factors in constraining EBP adoption. It is believed that EBP practices generally require a lot of resources, and may also entail training costs and the purchase of new equipment. As funding given to public sector organizations is heavily scrutinized, police agencies tend to avoid high-cost projects like EBP to avoid lowering their chances of securing these funds. However, a hotspots experiment by Telep et al (2014) with Sacramento Police Department in the USA revealed that EBP practices could be effectively adopted without entailing extra costs if the leadership was supportive and made innovative use of existing resources. While lack of financial resources may be an issue, it seems that the lack of time in the adoption of EBP is an even greater problem. In addition, the lack of expert staff poses a significant challenge, thereby adversely impacting EBP adoption. Consequently, officers struggling to respond to calls for service tend to face competing demands and excessive workload when tasked to complete further assignments, leading to resistance to new initiatives.

Another important factor leading to resistance towards EBP is the strained relationship between police officers and researchers. There exists a strong apprehension and scepticism in police organizations regarding the extent to which academics actually understand policing. Members of the police perceive outsiders as lacking the capacity to truly understand the difficulties inherent in their work. However, it is not scientific proof that police officers doubt but rather the validity of generalizations (Sherman, 2013). Resistance of EBP is aimed at protecting the work of policing as a craft so as to prevent researchers from interfering in their practices. Police organizations are slow to implement research evidence because researchers are perceived as focusing more on developing policies and far less on producing research that can be applied in practice.

The tensions between police officers and researchers also arise from a lack of consensus regarding the time needed to complete projects, the defining of issues, and measuring outcomes. Police officers are accustomed to making decisions on the fly, which does not align with the detail-oriented, time-consuming practices followed by researchers. Police agencies find it especially frustrating when reports are produced without their input. Such research is dismissed as being overly generalized and misinformed with recommendations that are incomplete, impractical, or impossible to implement. Bradley and Nixon (2009: 423) describe this kind of communication as the 'dialogue of the deaf', as it breeds resistance to adoption of EBP.

Finally, an important factor in the external organizational environment that leads to resistance to EBP is political interference. Interestingly the role of oversight bodies is both a facilitator and barrier to EBP, as discussed in the previous section on receptivity to EBP. It depends on how effectively police organizations present the case for EBP to these bodies. Due to their reliance on external funding, police agencies are at times compelled to adopt initiatives that do not serve organizational needs or that are not in line with their capacity. Such initiatives run the risk of being resisted by the implementing officers. Oversight bodies do not display an interest in new initiatives by police organizations when the latter are unable to showcase the usefulness of their own EBP ventures. In Canada, for example, police boards wield strong influence over police services in the provinces with particular reference to appointing police chiefs, delineating strategic direction, and controlling the budget. These boards tend to interfere in police affairs when the police organizations cannot demonstrate the capacity to undertake evidence-based decision-making. Mastrofski and Willis (2010) argue that such pressures can compel police organizations to exercise excessive caution in EBP implementation so as to avoid losing funding by external funding agencies.

Summing up

With the growing pressure to adopt evidence-based practices, police organizations must focus their attention on addressing the factors responsible for resistance to such practices. For the past two decades, scholars in policing have supported the idea of EBP adoption for the enhancement of organizational efficiency and effectiveness (Lum et al, 2012). This chapter helps us conclude that organizational context, that is, the internal and external environment of police agencies, can provide some sense of the barriers and facilitators of EBP. External pressure, interorganizational networking, organizational knowledge, and leadership support, along with a culture and climate supportive of change, can help embed evidence-based practices in police organizations. In terms of resistance to EBP, we have identified lack of communication within the organization, organizational culture, tangible and intangible resources, trust issues with researchers, and political interference as important factors. The measures to reduce resistance and enhance receptivity to EBP will be discussed in Chapter 8.

2

Situating evidence-based policing

Prior to the 1990s, policing across the West was largely conducted through what is known as the 'standard model' of policing (Sherman, 2013). This model, also known as the '3Rs', was a 'one-size-fits-all' reactive approach that placed heavy emphasis on *random* patrols, *rapid* responses to calls for service, and *reactive* investigations, along with intensive enforcement in the form of police crackdowns and/or saturation policing (Weisburd and Eck, 2004; Sherman, 2013). Despite the apparent popularity of such approaches within policing and political circles, widespread crime rate increases throughout the 1970s and 1980s led some to question the ability of the police to reduce and prevent crime (Bayley, 1994).

Growing doubt about the effectiveness of current policing styles, coupled with a growing body of evidence showing that practices under the standard model had little-to-no impact on crime (Skogan and Frydl, 2004), led to a period of significant innovation within policing. While the standard model was not replaced entirely, new policing processes and philosophies were developed and implemented. These innovations included not only evidence-based policing (EBP), but also problem-oriented policing (POP), community-oriented policing (COP), CompStat (Computerized Statistics) and intelligence-led policing (ILP).

One of the questions we are not infrequently asked is, 'What is the difference between EBP and POP?' Another is 'Does EBP replace COP?' Given the extent to which there is some overlap among these philosophies, and thus some natural confusion about whether they compete or complement one another, we thought it would be helpful to highlight some of the main characteristics and differences, focusing primarily on how each of these philosophies can be made compatible with an EBP approach. Thus, the purpose of this chapter is to situate EBP next to these other policing innovations.

To begin, this chapter will provide an overview of EBP, further expanding on its origins and what Sherman (1998) ultimately intended for it to solve. The focus of the chapter then shifts towards three unique, but complimentary, policing innovations – problem-oriented policing, community policing, and intelligence-led policing – to outline where EBP stands relative to them.

Evidence-based policing

As mentioned, Sherman's (1998) foundational piece for the National Police Foundation in the USA was the first to bring about the notion of policing being informed by empirical evidence. Inspired by earlier developments within the medical field, which itself experienced a paradigm shift toward evidence-based medicine, he defined EBP as using '... research to guide practice and evaluate practitioners. It uses the best evidence to shape the best practice. It is a systematic effort to parse out and codify unsystematic "experience" as the basis for police work, refining it by ongoing systematic testing of hypotheses' (Sherman, 1998: 4). In other words, EBP was put forth as an idea to replace the incorrect 'facts' that at times arise from an over-reliance on experience, intuition, and craft-based thinking, subsequently putting empirical evidence – generated through the ongoing systematic testing of research ideas – in its place (Sherman, 1998). This is not to say that experience, intuition, or craft-based thinking should be entirely disregarded within the context of EBP, but rather that it should not be the sole driving factor behind implementing a particular strategy, policy, or program (Willis and Mastrofski, 2018).

As may be recalled from this book's Introduction, the systematic testing of ideas within the context of EBP is done through what is known as the 'triple-T' strategy: *targeting, testing*, and *tracking* (Sherman, 2013). *Targeting* refers to the identification of a high-priority problem onto which a strategy is employed in order to address it. Said strategy should be *tested* through rigorous methods to ensure the desired outcome is achieved and *tracked* over time to ensure the desired outcome(s) continue(s). In the event that the desired outcome(s) is/are not being achieved, the strategy should be adjusted, followed by the *testing* and *tracking* of the adjustments (Sherman, 2013). This process leads us to an understanding of 'what works' when it comes to various policing strategies, policies, or programs, and thus a more effective and efficient use of already scarce police resources (Sherman, 2013; Heaton and Tong, 2016). One-off evaluations, however, do not deem something as being 'evidence-based'. Rather, an evidence base is established through replicated or reproduced research on the same strategy, policy, or program. As the results of each replication or reproduction are generated, we not only become increasingly confident as to whether the strategy, policy, or program 'works' (or not), but we also begin forming its respective 'base' of evidence (Huey and Bennell, 2017).

Relative to other policing innovations, Sherman (1998) argues that EBP is unique for several reasons. First, he argues that no other innovation contains the principles for its own implementation. In other words, since EBP uses evidence to evaluate and change police practice, evidence can similarly be used to evaluate the implementation of EBP. Second, no other innovation contains principles for the evaluation of police practice and adjusting practice based on the findings of the evaluation. Third, generated evidence can be used to hold practitioners accountable. Finally, and arguably most important as it relates to the context of this chapter, EBP is *helpful* to other innovations (Sherman, 1998). In other words, EBP is not meant to replace or be interpreted as an alternative to other policing innovations (Eck, 2019). Instead, EBP should be employed *alongside* them (Lum and Koper, 2017). In this way, irrespective of the innovations that are employed by a police service, EBP should be used to inform them based on the evidence that has already been generated and/or through in-house *targeting*, *testing*, and *tracking*.

Problem-oriented policing and evidence-based policing

One of the truisms of policing is that many, if not all, of the crime and disorder issues that become 'police property', and thus just criminal justice matters, are driven by community and social issues that could be prevented or better addressed through some creative problem-solving. With this view in mind, in 1979 criminologist Herman Goldstein created the concept of 'problem-oriented policing' (POP). Subsequently, Goldstein (2001) summarized the POP approach as follows:

1. *Discrete pieces of police business* (each consisting of a cluster of similar incidents, whether crimes or acts of disorder, that the police are expected to handle) are subject to
2. *Microscopic examination* (drawing on the especially honed skills of analysts and the accumulated experience of operating field personnel) in hopes that what is freshly learned about each problem will lead to discovering a
3. *New and more effective strategy* for dealing with it. POP places a high value on new responses that are
4. *Preventative* in nature, that are
5. *Not dependent on the use of the criminal justice system*, and that
6. *Engage other public agencies, the community and the private sector* when their involvement has the potential for significantly contributing to the reduction of the problem. POP carries commitment to
7. *Implementing the new strategy*,
8. *Rigorously evaluating its effectiveness*, and subsequently,
9. *Reporting the results* in ways that will benefit other police agencies and that will ultimately contribute to
10. *Building a body of knowledge* that supports the further professionalization of the police.

As can be seen from the tenets of POP listed above, it is considered to be a crime prevention *process* as opposed to a single policing strategy.

Given the evidence that has been generated on POP to date, we know that the general approach of targeting problems is effective at reducing crime and disorder (Weisburd and Eck, 2004;

Braga et al, 2015, 2019a). Even practices that are already deemed as evidence–based approaches for crime and disorder reduction, such as hotspots policing, are additionally enhanced when implemented within a POP context (Braga et al, 2014b; Braga and MacDonald, 2019). Simply put, this is because, instead of simply treating a hotspot with a saturated police presence in an effort to deter crime and/or disorder (see, for example, Ratcliffe et al, 2011), the underlying issues that lead to problems within the hotspot are targeted through the POP process (Eck and Spelman, 1987).

One of the most common frameworks through which POP is executed in practice is the SARA model (see Figure 2.1), developed by Eck and Spelman (1987). This model involves *scanning* and identifying problems; conducting an *analysis* of the identified problems for their respective underlying causes; creating a *response* that seeks to address the underlying causes of the problem(s), thus preventing it from occurring in the future; and executing an *assessment* on the response. In short, built within this model – and within the POP approach more generally – is some of the same key elements of the EBP approach, in particular its emphasis on *targeting, testing,* and *tracking.* So how are they not the same thing?

Figure 2.1: The SARA model

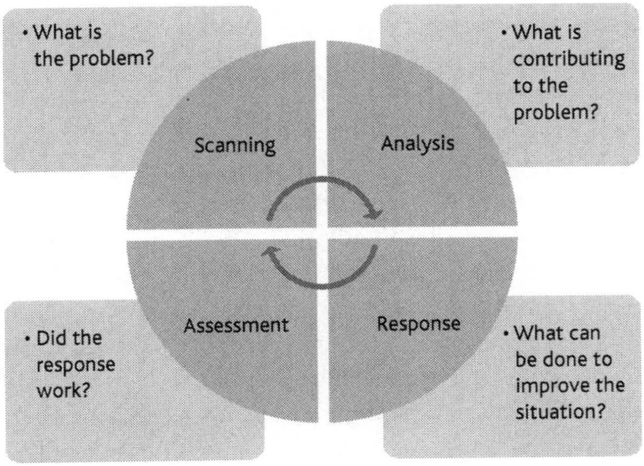

Source: Authors' own

One key area in which these two approaches differ is in their scope: whereas POP is primarily focused on crime prevention, EBP is a more holistic philosophy that can be used to tackle a much broader range of issues internal and external to a police service. Among such issues might include how to develop more effective recruitment strategies, evaluating promotional processes, implementing a procedural justice program to address internal complaints, testing more effective social media strategies, and increasing the effectiveness of police responses to missing persons cases, among others. Another way in which to think about how they differ is to remember that whereas POP is oriented around the question of 'how do I solve this problem?', EBP is centered on the broader question of 'what works?' The former approach assumes that something isn't working and thus requires a solution, whereas the latter allows for the possibility that something is working and should therefore be replicated (with appropriate testing and tracking).

Having emphasized how these philosophies differ, it is important to stress that these are not competing approaches. Instead, we see them as two sides of the same coin, with EBP complementing the use of POP in addressing local crime and disorder issues. What do we mean? The SARA model that is central to the POP approach relies heavily on the use of crime data and crime analysis to identify problems and generate feedback on how well an intervention is performing. Overreliance on crime data and conventional responses to local problems (such as policing crackdowns) can result in what has been viewed as 'shallow POP' (Bullock and Tilley, 2009). With 'shallow POP', a problem has been identified, but, given the limitations of relying solely or largely on crime data to identify and address problems, can we really say we have a detailed understanding of the true nature of the problem, including its root causes and/or local reactions to potential police interventions? And, without that detailed understanding, can we say the problem has really been 'solved' rather than temporarily or spatially displaced? In other words, did that targeted enforcement 'really work?' It is here that EBP can complement POP approaches by offering an array of different tools and methods for tackling not only 'what works' but also 'what caused this situation to happen.' Although there has been a strong emphasis on the use of RCTs by some researchers working within the EBP tradition, a more holistic view of EBP recognizes that diverse research questions require diverse methods for improving our understanding of how to really tackle problems.

Community-oriented policing and evidence-based policing

Community-oriented policing (COP), which began to gain significant traction in the policing community in the late 1980s, is, like EBP, neither a program, strategy, and policy, nor even a process; rather, COP is an overarching policing philosophy meant to guide all external operations of a police organization (Goldstein, 1987; Skogan and Frydl, 2004). Although definitions of COP vary, as do views of its key elements,[1] a common understanding of this philosophy has it resting on three fundamental tenets: community involvement, decentralization, and problem-solving (Skogan, 2019).

In relation to its first pillar, *community involvement*, COP places an expectation on the police to forge active partnerships with communities and local groups aimed at identifying and addressing crime and disorder issues of importance to residents. As part of this process, the public are no longer passive recipients of police expertise and services, but rather, actively engaged in defining problems and suitable responses, as well as establishing policing priorities. This co-production of solutions not only enables relationships to be built between the police and the community, but also allows the police to become more informed about issues that are important to community members, which is especially important given that some community-defined problems may not appear within police data (for example, various forms of disorder).

The act of forging partnerships with the community requires police services to become more accessible to community members, which is facilitated through the second COP pillar, *decentralization*. This pillar is concerned with 'flattening' the traditional police hierarchy by moving authority and responsibility downwards to the beat level (Skogan, 2019). To illustrate: in an ideal version of this, mid-level police managers have the authority and responsibility of COP within their areas, tasking frontline supervisors with directing and/or supporting the local community engagement efforts of their frontline officers. In turn, frontline officers assigned to specific communities serve to identify and construct solutions to problems that are raised by community members. This decentralized process stands in sharp contrast to other models, such as CompStat, in which decision-making has largely been driven at managerial level with very little input from the frontlines (Eterno and Silverman, 2012).

The third and final pillar of COP is *problem-solving*. Under the COP umbrella, problem-solving is centered on identifying and responding to community-defined 'problems'. In this regard, COP problem-solving can be very different from POP problem-solving: whereas COP is intended to focus on solving issues of importance to the community, POP problems are typically police-defined, with little community involvement. That said, both problem-solving processes can incorporate and do use the SARA model (Eck and Spelman, 1987).

As is the case with POP, EBP is not a competing framework, but rather one that can play a vitally important role in supporting the COP philosophy. We feel that it is incredibly important to emphasize this point because, as we have noted before, research has shown that some officers are resistant to EBP, fearing it will replace community policing and remove them from communities:

> I am a huge advocate of not removing policing agencies from close contact with the community it serves. There must be a balance. Removing oneself from community stakeholders to "hide" behind a computer is, in my opinion, a flawed strategy. (quoted in Huey et al, 2017: 552)

How might EBP help police services that are actively engaged in community policing? As with POP, an EBP approach can generate evidence on 'what works' and what does not. In relation to community policing, this would be a highly important task. In preparing this book, we reviewed a number of significant studies on COP. Of these, we note there have been four separate evidence reviews, which have summarized efforts to date and synthesized findings (Sherman and Eck, 2002; Skogan and Frydl, 2004; Gill et al, 2014; Weisburd and Majmundar, 2018).[2] Each of these reviews has arrived at similar conclusions:

- The methodological rigor of many COP studies is weak.
- COP has little-to-no direct impact on crime.[3]
- COP can increase citizen satisfaction with the police and reduce citizen perceptions of disorder.

What EBP could contribute to community policing is a stronger empirical framework through which to: (1) enhance understanding of community problems; (2) develop solutions; (3) evaluate interventions; and (4) track processes over time.

To support our argument that these two philosophies can, and ideally should, go together, we need only look at the recent slate of experiments on the use of procedural justice approaches to police–citizen interactions. Procedural justice (PJ) has been defined as a perspective that treats the legitimacy of the police as directly impacted by 'public judgments about the fairness of the processes through which the police make decision sand exercise authority' (Sunshine and Tyler, 2003: 514). Thus, 'if the public judges that the police exercise their authority using fair procedures, this model suggests that the public will view the police as legitimate and will cooperate with policing efforts' (Sunshine and Tyler, 2003: 514). Conversely, perceptions of unfair treatment by the police will lead to 'alienation, defiance, and noncooperation' (Sunshine and Tyler, 2003: 514). Although not directly related to the key tenets of COP as listed above, like COP strategies in general, PJ is aimed at enhancing police legitimacy and citizen satisfaction with police performance.

Employing the use of the PJ approach to a variety of citizen–police interactions – from routine traffic stops to counter-terrorism activities – researchers have consistently found a number of positive outcomes from its use (see Engel, 2005; Tyler et al, 2010). In a systematic review conducted by Lorraine Mazerolle and colleagues (2013), they found the inclusion of at least one element of the PJ model in relation to how police interacted with the public had significant impacts on both 'satisfaction with the police' and 'confidence in the police'. They also observe that some studies reported crime reduction effects as a result (Mazerolle et al, 2013). What makes such work a perfect example of the blending of the COP and EBP philosophies is the fact that much of this research has been undertaken from an explicitly EBP focus, including the use of standardized EBP methodologies, such as RCTs and meta-analysis (more of which will be discussed in the next chapter). In short, interventions aimed at enhancing community–police relations, improving crime prevention, and, ideally, those that do both, are exactly the types of applied policing issues that EBP advocates and researchers are keen to undertake, and they are also the types of issues with which COP practitioners must grapple. Simply put, blending the two approaches, as those working within the PJ field have done, just makes good sense.

CompStat

CompStat is a significant policing innovation of the 1990s, first developed in New York under the tenure of then NYPD Commissioner William Bratton (Vito et al, 2005). Combining strategic management principles with data-driven analysis, CompStat has been defined as 'a combined technical and managerial system that seeks to develop a certain kind of focused internal accountability in a police department' (Moore, 2003: 471). CompStat is based on four key principles that, combined, are centered on delivering strategic police responses to current and emerging local crime conditions. These principles include: accurate, timely information made available at all levels in the organization; the most effective tactics for specific problems; rapid, focused deployment of resources to implement those tactics; and relentless follow-up and assessment to learn what happened and make adjustments (Bratton, cited in Willis et al, 2007: 147).

How exactly does CompStat operate? Police organizations pursuing this approach typically invest in supporting data-driven approaches, from the employment of cutting-edge crime analysis tools to highly qualified staff with expertise in crime analysis, geographical information systems, predictive software, and so on. Crime data is carefully analysed to produce timely 'snapshots' of local trends, analyses that are delivered to police leaders and middle managers, the latter of whom are specifically tasked with responding to crime changes in their jurisdictions. Data is not only an indicator of actual and potential crime problems; it is also a performance tool. Embedded in the CompStat model is the clear expectation that police leaders will hold middle managers accountable for failures to drive down crime in their areas (Bratton and Malinowski, 2008).

With its focus on data-driven and problem-solving approaches to crime control, it would be easy to see how CompStat could be confused with EBP. Indeed, we have seen examples in professional journals of instances where the two were conflated, as though they were the same. Although they can be employed in various complementary ways, there are significant differences. For one thing, data is not the same thing as evidence. When one of us, Laura, teaches, EBP she uses the following slide to illustrate (see Figure 2.2):

Figure 2.2: The difference between data and evidence

Hrm. What about data? What's the difference between data and evidence? Why can't I just use my data?

- Data is just data and has no meaning on its own.

- Evidence is an interpretation of data – it has to be evidence for or of something; an argument, an opinion, a point of view or, if you wish to be all science-y, a hypothesis.

- You can think of it this way:

  What's the difference between a clue and evidence in policing?

Source: Authors' own.

The point of this slide is simple: scientific evidence comes with a set of interpretations of the data that are typically derived from a body of research – that is, from a set of proven or emergent theories that have been tested elsewhere. Say, what?

If we tell you that our data shows that 15 percent of adults aged 21–25 will have something stolen from them in a bar, what can you do with that fact? You might start thinking about some crime programs you could run, right? How about if we told that you there is a body of research that shows that not only will 15 percent of adults aged 21–25 have something stolen from them in a bar, but that the presence of capable guardians in that location observing the tables can reduce that number to 4 percent? Which of those two statements do you find more useful? I think we can guess. The first statement is data; the second statement is evidence (in the research context). The example Laura uses involving clues versus evidence operates in a similar way: a clue is only a clue until a detective creates an interpretation of that clue in relation to the body of evidence – the case – they are building.

Another way in which CompStat and EBP are very different is in relation to focus. The CompStat model is singularly focused on crime control. While it has been the case that EBP practitioners have paid significant attention to date on crime control efforts, EBP is not exclusively focused on these efforts. Indeed, a growing number of researchers working under the EBP umbrella are tackling issues that have little direct connection with crime suppression or responding to crime. Such efforts include examining efforts at improving police–LGBTQ+ community relations, and identifying effective strategies for searching for missing persons, among others.

All of the above notwithstanding, we want to be clear to note that while EBP and CompStat are not synonymous, they can work well together. What EBP can contribute to organizations employing the CompStat model includes, but is not limited to:

- Providing a broader empirical and theoretical base for understanding crime trends.
- Providing a framework for testing policing interventions to ensure they actually 'work' and that crime drops are not random or the result of other factors.
- Understanding the impacts of certain law enforcement interventions on local communities.

In short, employing an EBP approach with a CompStat model can help turn data into evidence, thus providing decision-makers with a deeper level of understanding and a wider array of tools for not only dealing with crime, but also with the panoply of other issues police services face.

Intelligence-led policing and evidence-based policing

The final innovation discussed here is intelligence-led policing (ILP). ILP arose to prominence as a policing philosophy in the UK in the late 1990s as a result of changes in how police services respond to organized crime. Recognizing the utility of pro-active intelligence gathering for dealing with other forms of inter and trans-jurisdictional threats – including riots and terrorism – ILP was widely adopted (Carter and Carter, 2009). What is ILP? It has been defined as:

> Intelligence-led policing emphasises analysis and intelligence as pivotal to an objective, decision-making framework that prioritises crime hotspots, repeat victims, prolific offenders and criminal groups. It facilitates crime and harm reduction, disruption and prevention through strategic and tactical management, deployment, and enforcement. (Ratcliffe, 2016: 66)

Similar to POP, CompStat and COP, ILP is not simply a policing strategy or approach, but rather a philosophy in which criminal intelligence and crime analysis drive decision-making processes as they relate to the *effective* allocation and execution of police resources. In practice, the execution of the ILP philosophy can be understood through Ratcliffe's (2016) 3i model. According to this model, officers on the frontline and crime analysts work to *interpret* the criminal environment, gathering and analysing information on identified problems. This information is subsequently used to *influence* decision-makers within the police organization, who then *impact* the criminal environment by employing evidence-based strategies that seek to reduce or prevent crime (Ratcliffe, 2016).

Relative to the other policing innovations discussed here, it is evident that ILP can be employed alongside either COP and/or POP. For instance, under a broader COP philosophy, intelligence can be collected from members of the community, which is subsequently *interpreted* and used to *impact* the criminal environment through a POP crime prevention strategy. ILP is especially complimentary to that of POP because intelligence can seamlessly aid in all stages of the POP process (Eck and Spelman, 1987; Ratcliffe, 2016). Where some confusion may arise is in relation to CompStat, an approach with which there appears to be significant overlap with ILP (Wood and Shearing, 2007). In their analysis of ILP, Carter and Carter (2009) argue they are also different in terms of a number of functional aspects. Chief among these is the fact that the primary focus of ILP 'is typically multijurisdictional and often complex criminality, such as criminal enterprises', whereas CompStat is an approach that is very much centered on local crimes (Carter and Carter, 2009).

How is ILP similar to or different from EBP? As we have observed in relation to CompStat, EBP is a holistic philosophy that promotes the development of scientific knowledge to answer a wide array of questions that affect policing. It is not solely centered on crime prevention or responses to criminality. Nor is data and its analysis the backbone that drives EBP, as is the case with ILP and CompStat. Although ILP practitioners may be interested in the underlying dynamics that generate domestic and international terrorism, as an example, understanding the WHY of criminality is of less interest than focusing on the HOW and, particularly, the question of HOW best to effect detection and prevention.

There are various ways in which EBP can complement ILP use within police services. For example, whereas impacting crime through empirically tested strategies aimed at its prevention is a hallmark of the 3i model, an EBP approach can provide additional value through the inclusion of a tracking component – that is, interventions are not only tested but also monitored and adjusted as required. Further, we note that, beyond the *impact* portion of the 3i model – which can easily draw on the evidence base of approaches that are already known to 'work', such as hotspots policing, POP, or focused deterrence – little is known about the effectiveness of ILP components, or even how ILP components complement one another in practice. Only recently have scholars begun looking at the organizational factors related to ILP implementation (see, for example, Darroch and Mazerolle, 2013; Carter, 2016) or how frontline intelligence gathering even impacts case outcomes (Bottema and Telep, 2019). Given the limited evidence base on ILP more generally, the *targeting*, *testing*, and *tracking* of *interpreting*, *influencing*, and *impacting* is especially important and requires study to enhance implementation and professional practice. Such research may involve examining many processes that are dependent on ILP, such as determining the best sources of intelligence, who should be responsible for obtaining it, how it should be obtained, and how it should be analysed. In short, EBP can help aid understanding on 'what works' in relation to ILP.

Summing up

The period from the late 1980s to the early 2000s saw the development of a number of significant innovations within contemporary policing, including POP, COP, CompStat and ILP, among others. It was also within this period that Sherman (1998) posited the notion of policing not being based on experience or intuition, but rather on empirical evidence. While the use of some of these innovations certainly calls for decisions to be made as to which innovation to employ over another, this is not the case with EBP.

As described throughout this chapter, EBP should not be mistaken for an alternative to other police innovations. Instead, EBP could be employed as a companion to them. Consulting the already-generated evidence on innovations can ensure that police services employ them in the most effective way possible. However, if there is a lack of evidence on a particular innovation – such as ILP, for example – Sherman's (2013) 'triple-T' strategy becomes paramount in ensuring that local evidence is generated on the innovation, thus generating knowledge as to whether the use of the innovation was effective or not.

3

Understanding research

Although we recognize that 'research methods' is often the least favourite topic for many people, successfully engaging with the 'triple-T' strategy – particularly as it relates to the *testing* component – requires a degree of knowledge on research methods and research design. In recognizing that engaging in research is not something that many police practitioners do as part of their regular duties, the purpose of this chapter is to provide an overview of research fundamentals.

To begin, this chapter will provide a broad overview of both quantitative and qualitative methods. While doing so, practical police-related examples will be provided to articulate how some of the elements discussed throughout can be employed in practice to answer research questions that may be pertinent within a policing context. Before wrapping up, we will also discuss two important components that are used to understand the body and quality of research: evidence hierarchies and evidence syntheses. As will be outlined later on, evidence hierarchies and syntheses not only help us in determining whether a particular police practice, policy, or strategy is evidence-based or not, but they also remind us to be cautious about what we consider as 'evidence'.

A note of caution: what this chapter will *not* do is explain *how* to employ what is discussed. Doing so would require significant elaboration on research-related components that simply cannot be described in full within a single chapter. Therefore, this chapter should be considered as a preliminary 'starting point' for basic information related to quantitative and qualitative methods.

Research questions and hypotheses

One of the most crucially important components of research is formulating a clear idea of what it is that you intend to study. A research question is *anything* that you seek to answer through your research, and the reason as to why establishing this component is so crucial is because the type of question you pose will impact *how* you approach your research from the beginning (Hesse-Biber and Leavy, 2011; White, 2017). For example, questions that are related to numbers – such as, 'how much has violent crime gone down on Main Street relative to similar areas?' – will mean that you will be engaging in quantitative methods. On the other hand, research questions that are related to an individual's interpretation or meaning – such as, 'what has been your experience working within the community for the last 10 years?' – will more often than not rely on qualitative methods.

The need for clarity cannot be understated. Carefully identifying what you seek to answer through your research will not only enable you to choose the most appropriate method to answer the question, but it will also ensure that you are focused on accurately measuring what you set out to measure (White, 2017). For example, questions such as, 'do police-led interventions on Main Street between First and Second Avenue work at reducing crime?', are ones to avoid. As the question is currently stated, it would be assumed that one would be measuring the impact of police interventions on crime on this section of Main Street. However, the key component that is missing from the question is, *which* interventions? Proceeding as is opens the possibility of different interventions being included in the study, each of which could be swapped in and out at any point throughout. Therefore, even *if* there is a reduction in crime on this section of Main Street after using several different interventions, you would be unable to say *which* interventions contributed to the reduction and which did not. Being extremely specific with your research question, such as, 'does a foot patrol on Main Street, between First and Second Avenue, reduce crime?', will allow you to stay focused throughout the study and therefore generate better results.

Hypotheses are a related component to research questions. Unlike research questions, however, a hypothesis is a statement that you make about what you *expect* the results of your study to show (Weisburd and Britt, 2014). For example, 'citizens who have positive interactions with the police will have higher police satisfaction than those with negative interactions.' Hypotheses can be proven or disproven; therefore they are exclusively used with quantitative methods. Further, since hypotheses are a statement of what we expect our research results to show, they depend on prior knowledge – such as previous research – to inform our expectations (Weisburd and Britt, 2014). In situations where there is insufficient knowledge to form a hypothesis, the study will instead rely on a research question. Reformulating the above hypotheses, we can instead ask: 'do citizens who have positive interactions with the police have higher police satisfaction than those with negative interactions?'

Quantitative methods

Quantitative methods use numerical data and statistical methods to improve understanding of a phenomenon. With numbers being the sole focus of quantitative methods, you may be happy to know that there are – relative to qualitative methods, which will be further discussed below – far fewer methods of quantitative data collection. Among the most frequently used methods are surveys (Fowler, 2013). Surveys allow you to collect a large amount of information on a sample of your population with very little effort, especially since the conception of digital survey technologies (Salkind, 2010). Moreover, if a survey is not suitable for your research, quantitative data can also be collected by physically counting the number of times something occurs. For instance, disorder-related issues, such as littering, do not show up in police data. Therefore, in order to collect this data, one would need to go out and devise a scheme for counting forms of disorder (see, for example, Sampson and Raudenbush, 1999).

Data that is collected specifically for the purpose of your study – such as through surveys or self counting – is referred to as 'primary' data (Hox and Boeije, 2005). Alternatively, quantitative research can also be conducted on 'secondary' data – that is, data that was collected for a different purpose, but that can be sufficiently repurposed to answer the research question(s) (Hox and Boeije, 2005). For instance, data that is made available through government Open Data portals would be considered secondary data. Similarly, crime and calls for service data is collected for reasons outside of research but can certainly be used to answer a wide array of research questions.

Quantitative data – whether primary or secondary – is organized in variables (units of meaning that either have a numerical value or can have one assigned). For example, someone's age might be 35 and their gender might be coded as 1 (male), 2 (female), or 3 (other). In relation to crime data, the number of crimes that occur on a particular street can be one variable; temperature or time are examples of other variables. Ultimately, the broad objective of quantitative research is to use relevant variables in the data set to test research questions or hypotheses through the appropriate statistical methods. The selection of the appropriate methods can vary quite significantly and can depend on a whole host of factors, such as your research question/hypothesis or the state of your data. Of course, describing each of the possible statistical methods is not possible here; however, in the broadest sense, quantitative research falls into one of three research designs: (1) non-experimental; (2) experimental; and (3) quasi-experimental.

Non-experimental designs

This area of quantitative research, as the name suggests, is concerned with research that is not experimental in nature. Descriptive statistics – that is, statistics that seek to *describe* the phenomenon under study – would fall under this umbrella. Suppose you ask, 'what is the state of crime on Main Street, between First and Second Avenue, over the last 10 years?', there are numerous, rather intuitive things that can be done with your data to tell you more about crime on this section of Main Street.

For example, you can simply count the number – or frequency – of crimes that occurred on this section of Main Street over the 10-year period (Weisburd and Britt, 2014). Additionally, these counts can be aggregated by crime type, year, month, or even week. Doing so will also allow you to develop and visualize a crime trend for this section of Main Street, which will further enable you to see how crime has increased, decreased, or stayed the same over the 10-year period. Further, you may also calculate the mean – or average – number of crimes per crime type, year, month, and/or week (Weisburd and Britt, 2014). Ultimately, descriptive approaches allow you to see the state of crime on this section of Main Street.

Correlations are another example of non-experimental quantitative research. Simply put, correlations seek to measure the statistical relationship between two or more variables (Salkind, 2010). For example, if you ask, 'is there a relationship between temperature and the number of crimes on Main Street, between First and Second Avenue, over the last 10 years?', and there is a weak correlation between the two, that would suggest that the variables do not share a relationship. On the other hand, a strong correlation would suggest that the variables *do* share a relationship.

Strong correlations are, however, at times misunderstood as an indication that one variable causes another. This is *not* the case, and it is why you frequently hear that correlation does not imply causation (Altman and Krzywinski, 2015). Spurious correlations – which show a statistical relationship between two non-directly related variables – further support the need to avoid inferring causation from correlation. Take, for example, the relationship between ice cream sales and the number of people drowning in swimming pools: as ice cream sales increase, so do the number of drownings. Because these items are correlated, some may mistakenly believe that increased ice cream sales *cause* drownings in swimming pools. As is quite obvious, however, ice cream sales do not cause drownings. It is actually a third variable – in this case, the rise in temperature during warmer months – that leads to increased ice cream sales and drownings.

A third and final example of non-experimental quantitative research are approaches that examine the effect of one or more variables on another, such as regressions (Salkind, 2010).[1] For example, if we ask, 'what effect does temperature have on the number of crimes on Main Street, between First and Second

Avenue, over the last 10 years?', regressions can be used to measure the effect that temperature has on the number of crimes per year, month, or week. Importantly, just like correlations, regressions – as with most non-experimental designs – *cannot* determine causality; however, with experimental research, we can begin to explore this idea.

Experimental designs

One way of thinking about the difference between non-experimental and experimental research designs is that experimental designs introduce the use of an intervention and subsequently measure the impact of that intervention in terms of whether it achieved a particular outcome (Weisburd and Britt, 2014). One of the most common forms of experimental research designs is the randomized controlled trial (RCT), where a sample of, say, individuals or even neighbourhood blocks is randomly assigned into a treatment group (that is, receives the intervention) or a control group (that is, does not receive the intervention). Because this process is randomized in nature, if the intervention is seen to have made an impact, RCTs enable you to confidently conclude that the impact was likely caused by the intervention and nothing else (Weisburd and Britt, 2014).

In policing research, the number of randomized experiments has grown in recent decades, many of which have been conducted on place-based policing strategies (Braga et al, 2014a). Such studies, for example, pose a research question like: 'what is the impact of foot patrols on crime in crime hotspots?' Using an RCT to answer this question, you would first begin with identifying suitable hotspots for the intervention. If you identify 30, half would be randomly assigned to receive the treatment (that is, foot patrols) and the other half would be assigned to the control (that is, no foot patrols) (see Figure 3.1).

Experimental research, however, requires that both treatment and control groups – to a certain degree – be equivalent (Weisburd and Britt, 2014). The need for the two groups to be as similar as possible is so that, when the results are analysed, the predominant difference between the two groups is that one group received the intervention whereas the other did not.

Figure 3.1: Randomized controlled trial (RCT)

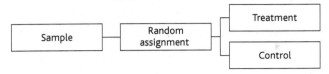

Source: Authors' own

However, even if efforts are made to balance the two, there will still be unknown differences between items or individuals in your sample. Fortunately, because the decision of who or what receives the intervention is up to chance, this means that everyone or everything in your sample has an equal chance of receiving the intervention. As a result, RCTs allow researchers to assume that any known or unknown differences are not influencing the outcome (Weisburd and Britt, 2014).

Quasi-experimental designs

Quasi-experimental methods are similar to experimental methods in that they involve employing an intervention and measuring its impact on an outcome. Where they differ is that quasi-experimental methods lack treatment randomization because it is either infeasible or unethical (Salkind, 2010). For example, if we return to our previous question, 'what is the impact of foot patrols on crime in crime hotspots?', if a jurisdiction is small enough, it is likely that they may only have a few hotspots, possibly even only one. In such a context, an experimental study is certainly not possible, but quasi-experimental studies are.

One of the most common forms of a quasi-experimental study is the pre- or post-test (see Figure 3.2). With this type of study, the level of crime in the hotspot would be measured

Figure 3.2: Pre- or post-test

Source: Authors' own

for a defined period before the intervention. Then, the hotspot would experience the foot patrol, and crime would subsequently be measured once more to examine whether the foot patrol had an impact on crime in the hotspot. If the level of crime decreases, we can conclude that the foot patrol *might* have contributed to the decrease. Unfortunately, however, due to the lack of randomization in quasi-experiments, we are less certain about whether it was the intervention that caused the impact on crime or whether it was some other factor (Weisburd and Britt, 2014).

For example, let us hypothetically assume that the crime in our one hotspot is largely driven by a very small group of individuals, but this information is not known to you. You plan a three-month foot patrol in the hotspot, which, also unbeknownst to you, coincides with the group temporarily re-locating for the same three-month period. The foot patrol is deployed, and the post-test reveals a crime decrease in the hotspot. Here it is easy to make the connection that the foot patrol resulted in the crime decrease, when, in fact, it was the temporary departure of the group that contributed to the decrease, not the foot patrol. This is certainly an exaggerated example, although it does explain one of the main limitations of quasi-experiments.

When possible, those conducting quasi-experiments should seek to use a control group. Doing so will not only improve your ability to determine whether your foot patrol *caused* a decrease in crime, but it will also enhance your ability to say that the foot patrol may have *contributed* to a crime decrease by comparing a location to a similar hotspot that received no treatment.

Qualitative methods

In contrast to the use of numbers and statistics in quantitative methods to answer research questions or to (dis)prove hypotheses, qualitative methods seek to gather individuals' interpretations and meanings as they relate to a particular research question (Seale, 1999; Hesse-Biber and Leavy, 2011). Interpretations and meanings are, at times, very specific to a particular context, and therefore cannot be used to make generalized statements (Hesse-Biber and Leavy, 2011). For example, one of our colleagues studies how gang-affiliated young men in Chicago in the USA use social media (Stuart, 2020). While there may be some similarities to, say, how adolescents in a Toronto suburb in Canada use YouTube or Instagram, clearly there will also be some very key differences that are rooted in the unique aspects of life in Chicago's Southside. Diving deep into the experiences of these young men through interviews and field observation allows the researcher to produce important insights that might not be gleaned in any other way.

Unfortunately, due to the aims of qualitative research, it is at times assumed to be a 'lesser' science than quantitative research, or not science at all (Seale, 1999). However, placing quantitative research above qualitative research, or vice versa, is the incorrect way of thinking about qualitative and quantitative research. Rather, they should be seen as two different approaches that can be used based on a given research question. If the research question involves numbers, then quantitative methods will be most appropriate; however, if the research question seeks to understand individuals' interpretation and meaning – such as, 'how has working on the frontlines impacted you?' – qualitative methods would be more appropriate.

With respect to qualitative data collection, the number of methods for collecting qualitative data outnumbers that of quantitative methods. This is because, while quantitative data is only concerned with numbers, qualitative data can involve speech, text, photos, and videos, among other sources (Lofland et al, 2006; Hammersley and Atkinson, 2007; Hesse-Biber and Leavy, 2011). Each of these sources of data can themselves be collected by various data collection techniques, leading to *many* different options for qualitative data collection. Here, I touch on some of the most common forms.

Interviews

Among all of the qualitative methods available, interviews are among the most common. This form of data collection can be conducted in-person, over the phone, or through digital means, and involves an interviewer posing questions to an interviewee (Hesse-Biber and Leavy, 2011). The questions asked during interviews are typically pre-determined and brought to the interview in the form of an interview guide (Lofland et al, 2006). However, interviews may reveal aspects about your research topic that were not initially known to you. Fortunately, qualitative research encourages you to explore these areas of your topic and to adjust your interview guide as you learn new things (Hammersley and Atkinson, 2007). Alternatively, interviews can also be conducted in a highly unstructured format, without an interview guide. These forms of interviews typically start with a broad question from the interviewer at the beginning, and transition into an informal conversation between the interviewer and interviewee about the topic at hand (Lee, 1993).

In a policing context, interviews can be employed to understand a whole host of matters. For example, if your service wants to understand why crime tends to occur within a particular area, conducting interviews with citizens and businesses around the hotspot can yield significantly important information behind some of the underlying factors that may contribute to crime in the said area. Among the various policing topics we have explored, using interviews as the primary method, we can include: peer support programs, women's experiences in policing, police recruitment, aspects of working in criminal investigation and forensic identification units, police experiences of trauma and resiliency, and technological challenges facing officers in special victims units.

Focus groups

Furthermore, interviews can also be conducted in a group format. These are commonly referred to as 'focus groups' or 'focused interviews' and involve a moderator – usually the interviewer – and a group of five to six participants (Morgan, 2004). Instead of posing questions to a single participant, questions are posed by the moderator to the group. While individual members of the group provide their responses, focus groups tend to develop what is known as a 'group dynamic'. As part of this dynamic, you can see and hear members of the group building on themes from one another, challenging and/or supporting one another, or even modifying their thoughts or views depending on what is said within the group (Morgan, 2004).

Returning to our hotspot example, employing focus groups to understand some of the underlying factors behind crime in an area can be especially beneficial. Instead of receiving one person's understanding of the area and what may or may not contribute to crime, focus groups allow you to develop multiple insights and to discover the extent to which these insights are shared across a group (or not). Focus groups are therefore useful to developing a more wholistic understanding of a phenomenon – from a neighbourhood hotspot to, say, the reluctance of some groups and individuals to report crimes.

Observation and ethnography

Qualitative data can also be collected through observation. This method of data collection can be particularly useful when you are tying to understand how a social phenomenon operates, without interfering with the setting or the individuals (Silverman, 2001; Hammersley and Atkinson, 2007). If interviews and focus groups are not feasible in understanding a crime hotspot, for example, observations can be used to develop a first-hand understanding of how or why crime may be occurring within the hotspot. Throughout this endeavour you could record your observations in writing, take photos, or even take videos (Hammersley and Atkinson, 2007; Hesse-Biber and Leavy, 2011).

A related approach that, in fact, a lot of early policing research used are ethnographies (Manning, 2014). Ethnographies involve getting close to a setting and the people within it. Researchers engaged in this type of research use interviews, observations, photographs, and documents, among other sources of information, to form an understanding behind the everyday life of the people within the setting as well as the setting itself (Hammersley and Atkinson, 2007; Hesse-Biber and Leavy, 2011). Admittedly, ethnographies require a significant time and resource investment; however, such work typically yields richer insights than other methods would allow.

Qualitative data from surveys

Although less frequently used in qualitative research, qualitative data can also be collected through analysing open-ended questions on surveys – in other words, by providing respondents with the space within which to expand on thoughts, perceptions, or feelings, researchers can potentially learn more than they might with only the results of closed-ended questions (that is, Y or N or scaled responses).

Evidence hierarchies

Now that you are a little more familiar with quantitative and qualitative research, it is important to emphasize that not all evidence is equal. Especially when it comes to decision-making within a policing context, it is crucial to draw on evidence that is not only credible, but that was also generated through high-quality, objective research – that is, studies need to be rigorous in nature (Morse et al, 2002). Decisions as to which evidence to rely on and which to avoid in a decision-making process can be aided through evidence hierarchies – the higher the evidence is on the hierarchy, the higher the rigor. Many evidence hierarchies have been developed to date; however, here we specifically expand on two: the first is Jerry Ratcliffe's evidence hierarchy from his recent book, *Reducing Crime: A Companion for Police Leaders* (2018), and the second is one that Laura developed for use in qualitative research.

Quantitative research hierarchy

In this section we describe Ratcliffe's (2020) 'Evidence hierarchy', a copy of which can be found on his *Reducing Crime* website (see www.reducingcrime.com/).

Beginning at the bottom of the hierarchy, level 0 provides examples of evidence that should never be relied on. Items such as anecdotes and opinion are pieces of evidence that Sherman (1998) wanted the police to move away from in the decision-making process. This is because these pieces of evidence are not even generated through research, but through experience or intuition. Based on a person's opinion, you can never be sure whether something 'works' or not. Similarly, commercial or internal reports – especially those that appear to have a conflict of interest – should also be avoided.

Levels 1 and 2 begin revealing evidence that is interesting but not necessarily suitable for basing a decision on. Studies without a control group or studies done in a retrospective nature would fall under these categories. As described above, while such studies may show that an intervention had an impact, these studies are unable to rule out the possibility of other factors – beyond the intervention – having an impact on the outcome. Retrospective studies also suggest that the researcher(s) may have had no control over who or what received the intervention, and in which way this decision was determined.

Levels 3 and 4 are items of evidence that are promising. Here, pre-/post-test studies with one or multiple comparisons groups can provide us with a better indication that the intervention had an impact on the outcome. Again, however, quasi-experimental studies are unable to rule out the possibility of factors beyond the intervention having an impact on the outcome. This is why RCTs are at the top of the hierarchy as they are able to tell us – with a high degree of certainty – whether an intervention 'worked' or not. This is also why RCTs are commonly referred to as the 'gold standard' of research (Sherman, 1998). Even higher above RCTs are two forms of evidence syntheses – systematic reviews and meta-analyses – discussed further below.

Qualitative research hierarchy

When it comes to qualitative evidence, opinions, anecdotes, or commercial evidence should also not be relied on in decision-making. This, again, is because this information is either generated through experience or intuition as opposed to empirical evidence, or because there may be a conflict of interest present in the work.

Unlike quantitative research, where scientists have tended to rate some methods as more rigorous than others – notably RCTs – qualitative researchers do not rank one method over

Figure 3.3: Huey's qualitative evidence hierarchy for policy decision-making

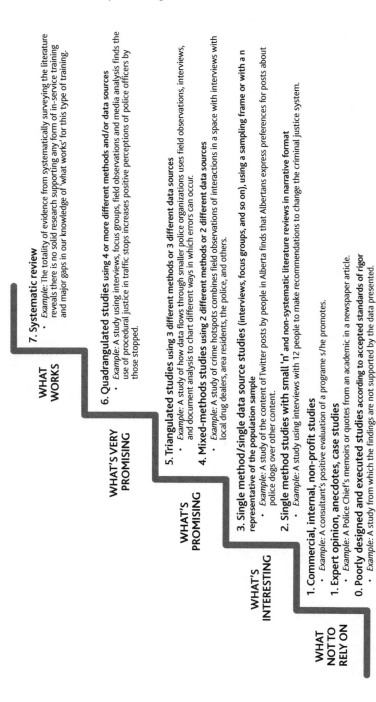

7. Systematic review
- *Example:* The totality of evidence from systematically surveying the literature reveals there is no solid research supporting any form of in-service training and major gaps in our knowledge of 'what works' for this type of training.

6. Quadrangulated studies using 4 or more different methods and/or data sources
- *Example:* A study using interviews, focus groups, field observations and media analysis finds the use of procedural justice in traffic stops increases positive perceptions of police officers by those stopped.

5. Triangulated studies using 3 different methods or 3 different data sources
- *Example:* A study of how data flows through smaller police organizations uses field observations, interviews, and document analysis to chart different ways in which errors can occur.

4. Mixed-methods studies using 2 different methods or 2 different data sources
- *Example:* A study of crime hotspots combines field observations of interactions in a space with interviews with local drug dealers, area residents, the police, and others.

3. Single method/single data source studies (interviews, focus groups, and so on), using a sampling frame or with a n representative of the population sample
- *Example:* A study of the content of Twitter posts by people in Alberta finds that Albertans express preferences for posts about police dogs over other content.

2. Single method studies with small 'n' and non-systematic literature reviews in narrative format
- *Example:* A study using interviews with 12 people to make recommendations to change the criminal justice system.

1. Commercial, internal, non-profit studies
- *Example:* A consultant's positive evaluation of a programe s/he promotes.

1. Expert opinion, anecdotes, case studies
- *Example:* A Police Chief's memoirs or quotes from an academic in a newspaper article.

0. Poorly designed and executed studies according to accepted standards of rigor
- *Example:* A study from which the findings are not supported by the data presented.

WHAT WORKS

WHAT'S VERY PROMISING

WHAT'S PROMISING

WHAT'S INTERESTING

WHAT NOT TO RELY ON

Source: Authors' own

another. Instead, qualitative studies that use multiple sources of data and/or multiple methods are considered to be of a higher quality than studies that use fewer data sources and/ or methods. While RCTs alone can indicate whether an intervention was effective or not, there is no single form of qualitative research or analysis that is able to do the same. This specific concern is known as 'internal validity'. Simply put, internal validity is concerned with the degree of truth behind research results (Seale, 1999). RCTs are high in internal validity because, again, the decision of who or what receives the intervention is due to chance, therefore allowing you to confidently conclude that if there was an impact, it was likely caused by the intervention and nothing else (Weisburd and Britt, 2014). In other words, we would consider results generated by RCTs to have a high degree of truth because other possible factors are ruled out.

Qualitative research, on the other hand, does not have a single method from which results are seen as more truthful than others. This is because, again, qualitative research is concerned with interpretation and meaning, which can vary from person to person. Truth, in the context of qualitative research, is therefore identified by triangulating it with multiple methods and data sources (Seale, 1999; Hesse-Biber and Leavy, 2011). In a geographical sense, you can use multiple landmarks to identify your position on a map; in a similar sense, you can use multiple qualitative methods or data sources to identify the truth (Seale, 1999). In this way, studies that use three or four methods or data sources are considered to be higher in rigor than studies that use one or even two methods or data sources.

Evidence syntheses

Evidence syntheses are useful for determining several things, such as how much research has been generated on a particular area, the quality of the evidence generated, and – most importantly – whether a particular policy, strategy, or program 'works'. While evidence syntheses take many different forms, we are focusing on three of the more common: scoping review, systematic review, and meta-analysis.

Scoping review

Scoping reviews are a type of evidence synthesis that attempts to broadly capture the body of research on a particular area. More specifically, scoping reviews can be used to capture the extent, range, and nature of research in an area, or to identify gaps where future research may be needed (Arksey and O'Malley, 2005). Importantly, before searching for literature to include in your scoping review, you need to establish a clear question or set of questions that you seek to answer through your review, and a clear and documented search strategy. As part of this search strategy you can identify numerous things, such as where you search for articles to include in your review, what terms you used in your search, and so on. Further, you may also identify a set of inclusion or exclusion criteria for your scoping review. Say, for example, that you are only interested in studies published between 2000 and 2019, this would be an inclusion criterion. Finally, you also need to establish how you will code or log the information that you wish to extract from the articles in your review. Having a clear analysis strategy will allow you to collect and organize the relevant information from your articles to answer your questions (Arksey and O'Malley, 2005). All these criteria need to be established before executing your search to minimize bias and to enable you to recreate your review if needed. Fortunately, scoping reviews are flexible in nature, so that as you become more familiar with the topic of research, you can refine your search strategy or inclusion/exclusion criteria as needed (Arksey and O'Malley, 2005).

One of us, for example, once used a scoping review to: (1) examine the nature and scope of Canadian policing research; (2) identify topics that were not represented within the Canadian policing research; and (3) what topics are missing entirely (Huey, 2016). It was found that over a 10-year period (2006–15), the number of papers published on Canadian policing was very low (n=188). The review also highlighted the fact that many topics that were significantly under-represented within Canadian policing research certainly require more research in the future (Huey, 2016).

Systematic review and meta-analysis

Systematic reviews are similar to scoping reviews in that they also require a clearly identified search strategy, inclusion and exclusion criteria, and a clear coding and analysis strategy of the included articles; however, this form of evidence synthesis is not flexible. That means that certain elements, such as the search strategy or inclusion/exclusion criteria, must be adhered to throughout the entire process. This is because systematic reviews are highly focused in nature and attempt to synthesize the findings on a particular policy, program, or intervention with as little bias as possible (Uman, 2011). As a result of their highly focused nature, systematic reviews are able to tell us about the quality of evidence on a particular policy, program, or intervention. Additionally, depending on the quality of evidence that is included, the systematic review may be able to determine whether the policy, program, or strategy 'works'. This is one reason why systematic reviews are situated at the top of both quantitative and qualitative evidence hierarchies.

In the policing context, systematic reviews have been conducted on several approaches to policing, such as hotspots policing (Braga et al, 2019b), problem-oriented policing (Weisburd et al, 2010), and community policing (Gill et al, 2014), among others. In their systematic review on hotspots policing, for example, Braga et al (2019b) sought to determine the effects that this policing strategy had on crime. After identifying 65 studies that were either an RCT or quasi-experimental in nature (that is, part of their inclusion criteria), they were able to determine that hotspots policing is an effective crime prevention strategy by the reductions in crime experiences across the included studies (Braga et al, 2019a).

Importantly, the researchers were able to come to this conclusion through the help of a meta-analysis. Meta-analyses are an added component to some systematic reviews where the authors want to summarize the quantitative results across all of the included. In other words, meta-analyses are a statistical procedure that is used to combine the individual quantitative results from each of the studies in the systematic review to come up with a single statistic on the effect of the policy, program, or strategy that is the focus of the review (Uman, 2011). For example, some of the studies included in Braga et al's (2019a) systematic review on hotspots policing examined the effect of the practice on specific crime types, such as violent crime, property crime, disorder, and drug offenses. They were able to summarize the quantitative findings for each of these crime types through a meta-analysis, finding that hotspots policing is effective at preventing each of these crime types.

Summing up

In an effort to *test* strategies that are executed against a *targeted* problem, both quantitative and qualitative research methods are vital tools throughout the testing process. Ultimately, the goal of testing – whether through quantitative or qualitative methods – is to generate evidence that contributes to our collective knowledge about 'what works' and what does not in the context of policing. Doing so provides a foundation through which policing policies, practices, and strategies can increasingly become based on empirical evidence, which can be further confirmed through evidence syntheses, such as systematic reviews and meta-analyses.

Importantly, however, not all forms of evidence are equal. Some, such as opinions and anecdotes, should be subjected to a high degree of scrutiny, whereas evidence generated through RCTs or quadrangulated qualitative work can confidently be relied on as these studies are very high in quality. Understandably, such high-quality evidence is not available for every aspect of contemporary policing. Therefore, where possible, decisions should be based on evidence from the next available level on the hierarchy, or it should be generated through the 'triple-T' strategy, targeting, testing, and tracking.

4

The individual approach

In the earliest days of evidence-based policing (EBP), it was an approach understood and adopted by only a handful of people, arguably a few academics and police leaders in the UK and USA. Today, much has changed. We are increasingly seeing its adoption by a range of policing practitioners and scholars across the globe. Among the former are *crime analysts* (Drawve et al, 2017; Finnegan et al, 2018; Mark et al, 2019), *frontline police officers* (Williams and Coupe, 2017), and *police leaders* (Martin, 2018; Murray, 2018), who are variously developing, executing, commissioning, and/or using research to inform policies and practices. Some of this work is beginning to occur at the agency level (most notably in the UK); however, EBP does not require a whole-agency approach, and many practitioners work on individual or one-off projects on their own, hoping to build internal and external support for evidence-based practices through success. Others adopt EBP simply because it suits their personal ethos, providing them with individual opportunities to solve problems within their work environment, and creating new opportunities to stimulate learning and personal growth.

Introducing a new way of critically examining policy and practice is uncomfortable for most professions. In policing, an occupational culture with a history of conservativism, traditionalism, and concern for rank and hierarchy (Skolnick, 1966; Loftus, 2010; Paoline, 2014), attempting to advance a scientific approach to the policing profession on your own can seem daunting[1] (see, for example, Reuss-Ianni, 1983; Chan, 1997). That said, there are some excellent resources on implementing small- or large-scale organizational changes that can help you to navigate these murky waters (see, for example, Grant, 2016; Kaplan, 2017). And in this chapter, we provide further assistance by including some concrete ideas from educational sources for getting started or continuing your journey to learning about and implementing EBP, as well as how to effectively network with researchers and other EBP practitioners.

Starting from scratch

Nowadays, when people want to know more about a topic, they often turn to the internet. While there are many advantages to 'surfing' for knowledge, this method is not without its limitations. Anyone in the discipline of Medicine will tell you, for example, that the field is rife with jokes about Doctor Google and patients using online websites to diagnose themselves with rare diseases. Professors often have to advise students that, while helpful for wining arguments with family members, Wikipedia is not a trustworthy academic source for your term paper. Although some judicious surfing may be helpful, in the sections that follow, we offer some practical (and more reliable) suggestions for getting started.

Books

Depending on the focus of a book, many academic books strive to synthesize the knowledge of the field into one document that anyone can access. Although the paywall that most academic literature sits behinds prevents many practitioners or laypeople from accessing information about research,[2] academic books get around this by offering a synopsis of the field within a book for a relatively low price. EBP is still a growing field, so the number of books on this specific topic is limited. Two authors of this book have edited a book on EBP titled *Evidence Based Policing: An Introduction* (Mitchell and Huey, 2018). This book gives an overview of what EBP is, examples of how it has been implemented in the field, and the challenges police agencies face when attempting to advance EBP in their organization. *Evidence Based Crime Prevention*, edited by Lawrence Sherman et al (2002), was one of the first books written about EBP. In it, the authors tied research to crime prevention strategies in an effort to get police practitioners to pay attention to the research (Sherman et al, 2002). The thought was, if EBP was tied to reductions in crime, the police as a profession might start to be more actively interested in police research. One of the first books to translate the research base into actionable practice was *Evidence-Based Policing: Translating Research into Practice* (Lum and Koper, 2017). The book includes a 'playbook', a more focused approach than Sherman et al (2002), to give police practitioners an implementation guide for specific EBP strategies. It reviewed what worked and what didn't in policing, and was a very thorough book covering all the advances in police research that had been made since *Evidence Based Crime Reduction* was published. The last book specifically addressing EBP is *Advances in Evidence-Based Policing* edited by Johannes Knutsson and Lisa Tompson (2017), focused on the type of research methodology academics were employing in the field and discussing the best approach to applying methodology.

Any of these books is a good place to start. They all describe what EBP is, how it has been applied in the field, and the challenges people have faced along the way. As you read through them, make note of the research that is referenced. If you are interested in a specific topic, look up the articles and read them, as this is a good way of gaining a more in-depth understanding of the field. If you don't have access, reach out to one of the authors, either through ResearchGate or email them and ask for a copy. Academics can share their work personally. If you are interested in conducting your own experiments, an online guide was co-authored by Renée Mitchell with Cody Telep and Cynthia Lum through George Mason University – *The Ten-Step Guide for Conducting In-House Experimental Evaluations* (Mitchell et al, 2017). This guide is free and located on George Mason University's Center for Evidence-Based Crime Policy.

Podcasts

There are plenty of podcasts related to policing, but be mindful that some are dedicated to discussions about issues in policing rather than research. For example, the US Department of Justice

COPS (Community Oriented Policing Services) Office has a podcast called *The Beat* (COPS Office, 2019). It covers a range of topics that affect policing. When reviewing the podcasts in their collections, most center round a discussion with a police executive in the field. These types of podcasts highlight that person's professional experience, which may or may not align with the current research. Police 1 in the USA has a podcast titled *Policing Matters*, where experts in the field are interviewed about their views on a specific topic (Wyllie and Dudley, 2019). *Quality Policing*, hosted by Professor Peter Moskos and practitioner Leon Taylor, focuses on police topics of interest around the USA such as officer-involved shootings, protests, and stop and search techniques (Moskos and Taylor, 2019). When reviewing podcasts, listen to a few episodes to determine whether the podcasts review relevant research or are more of a 'talking head' type.

Some podcasts focus entirely on police research. The *Criminal Justice Research* podcasts from the National Institute of Justice in the USA cover a broad spectrum of research issues affecting the criminal justice system (National Institute of Justice, 2019). These range from wrongful conviction to risk prediction to the neurobiology of sexual assault. They are informed by current research and can help to develop a specific area. *Crimeversation* in the USA is a podcast hosted by two doctoral students covering true crime, criminological and criminal justice issues while promoting research (Miley and Shreve, 2019). Their topics cover the hot issues in policing while at the same time inviting a lead scholar to discuss the research supporting the topic. They have been able to get top academics in the field to come on their show. The *How to EBP* podcast launched in the fall of 2019 by the Canadian Society of Evidence-Based Policing (Can-SEBP), hosted by Laura Huey and Vincenzo Soave, explores topics related to how to implement EBP within different types of police organizations, building from Laura's three-year Law Enforcement Advancing Data and Science (LEADS) Agencies Canada project with small- and medium-sized services. *Reducing Crime* is a podcast hosted by Dr Jerry Ratcliffe from Temple University in Philadelphia, Pennsylvania (Ratcliffe, 2018b). It focuses on academics doing research in the field and has an evidence-based focus (see Figure 4.1).

Figure 4.1: *Reducing Crime* podcast

#02: Mike Newman

Detective Inspector Mike Newman talks to me about his work introducing evidence-based policing to the Queensland Police Service in Australia, and the ways they have succeeded in embedding evidence-based practice into their agency.
Mike is one of the most well-known advocates of evidence-based policing, travelling widely to share his experiences working on the front-line of evidence-based practice and learning. I caught up with him at the Society of Evidence-Based Policing conference in Milton Keynes in the UK, in March 2018.

Mike has over 26 years' service, having worked general duties; crime units; criminal investigation; and a tactical unit. He has also been seconded to the Australian Crime Commission. In 2013, he managed the Mobile Police Community Office evidence-based policing project. Mike was promoted to Inspector in 2015 and was recently appointed as Detective Inspector over the Investigations and Intelligence Training Unit. In 2016 Mike undertook a 15-month secondment as the Evidence Based Policing Visiting Fellow at the University of Queensland where he worked with the renowned Professor Lorraine Mazerolle. He is the secretariat of the Australia and New Zealand Society for Evidence Based Policing, and a well-known advocate for EBP.

Reducing Crime
#02 (Mike Newman)

Source: Ratcliffe (2018b)

Podcasts are one way of improving knowledge about police research. They should be used cautiously as most hosts don't vet the comments of their interviewees, thus everything you hear from a podcast shouldn't be automatically believed. It should be followed up by reading the scientific literature. Trust, but verify.

Webinars

Many researchers, police services, trainers, police groups, consultants, and others have recognized the utility of webinars in reaching new audiences and, as a result, there are many, many webinars to choose from. The downside is that webinars, like podcasts, might be on general topics of interest, but not necessarily deliver informative, evidence-based content. Thus, it helps to pay attention to the source of the content being delivered. Is it from a respected researcher in the field? From an experienced practitioner who is familiar with the relevant research? It can be difficult to tell. However, we have some suggestions for you.

One of the first webinars on EBP was launched in 2018 by Can-SEBP and featured our own co-author, Renée Mitchell, as the very first guest. Since then, 12 more webinars have been produced, featuring experts talking on research on such diverse topics as: public perceptions of police officer dress, police–academic partnerships, hotspots policing, procedural justice, women in policing, use of force, police technology, and the role of crime analysis, among others.

Other webinars include those produced by the Strategies for Policing Innovation (SPI), which has conducted webinars on topics such as RCTs in criminal justice, Criminology 101 and 102, UK models of policing in SPI, body-worn cameras, and social network analysis (SPI, 2020). The webinars are conducted by researchers in the field, funded by the Bureau of Justice Assistance Smart Policing Initiative grant. They are informative, empirically accurate, and cover relevant and timely topics.

Justice Clearinghouse is a for-profit organization that was created to assist with the training of criminal justice professionals in the USA. Criminal justice organizations are often required by state or federal entities to have a designated number of hours of training a year or training on a specific topic. These are often costly to a criminal justice agency, either having to put on in-house training or send their employees elsewhere to receive the training. Justice Clearinghouse created a virtual conference for the criminal justice community to receive training via webinars (Justice Clearinghouse, 2019). Justice Clearinghouse is not specifically focused on the empirical evidence, but has recently begun to run a series of webinars hosting the National Institute of Justice's LEADS scholars who are focused on research related to policing. Additionally, Justice Clearinghouse has partnered with the American Society of Evidence-Based Policing (ASEBP) to host 12 EBP webinars yearly. These will focus on a range of topics to build the listeners' understanding of EBP: RCTs, EBP 101, statistical analysis for beginners, the role of crime analysts in EBP, EBP in the world, and other topics important to policing. The webinars will partner a practitioner with an academic to ensure research is their central focus.

Classes

Classes that will support an individual's EBP education are not just limited to EBP. There are classes that will help build an individual's understanding of criminological theory, statistics, crime analysis, or research methodology that are not marketed as an evidence-based course. However, they are still a good way to build up knowledge that supports evidence-based practices. One of the more intensive courses at the Inter-University Consortium for Political and Social Research (ICPSR) is the Summer Program in Quantitative Methods of Research (ICPSR, 2019). It is held at the University of Michigan in the USA and offers a wide variety of classes on statistics, research methodology, math concepts, and software such as Stata, RStudio, R, and SPSS. ICPSR offers courses for individuals no matter their level of expertise. They are offered in two formats: a four-week intensive course offered at the University of Michigan, or week-long workshops that are offered in the USA, Canada, and the UK. The week-long courses can build an individual's research capabilities in a very short period.

There are also classes offered in the UK, Australia, and New Zealand called 'masterclasses'. These are offered in a flexible format, ranging from one hour to one day. For example, Greater Manchester Police (GMP) has a five-day EBP masterclass – combining classroom learning with online tutorials – and to be accredited internally as an 'EBP champion', you must have successfully completed the course. Other courses on EBP are offered through the University of Queensland in Australia in partnership with the Queensland Police Service (QPS) for Australia and New Zealand, and across the UK, more generally, there are courses available through the College of Policing (2019b). The masterclasses focus on developing the police practitioner's ability to review, create, and implement research in practice. The class participants work in small groups, usually 5–10 people, through problems relevant to their organization. The course facilitators assist with developing theory-driven solutions that can be tested in the field. They walk practitioners through developing the appropriate research methodology for the question being asked. Additionally, participants learn how to manage case flows, monitor progress, and troubleshoot legal or ethical issues. The masterclasses are student-centered. The student (practitioner) brings the problem or issue to a class and the academic then uses this problem to teach scientific methodology in a step-by-step process. The students learn EBP by doing rather than listening. In the UK officers have access to masterclasses as an in-service training course and the UK College of Policing offers evidence-based camps. The EBP camps are a two-day course also aimed at increasing practitioners' knowledge of evidence-based approaches to policing issues. They specifically address: how and why to take an evidence-based approach, how to identify and explore policing problems, how to develop a targeted approach, and how to plan your own evaluation to test if your response 'works' (College of Policing, 2019a).

In 2021, the ASEBP will be launching a new four-week condensed course based on the structure of the University of Cambridge's Master of Studies (MSt) program (see below). Students will receive instruction on a diverse range of important topics, such as criminological theory, research design, and how to execute a research project. As they say, 'watch this space!'

College and university programs

The University of Cambridge's Police Executive Programme's MSt in Applied Criminology and Police Management is one of the only Master's programs in the world that teaches police executives how to apply research to their practices and to design high-level field research themselves (see www.crim.cam.ac.uk). This Master's degree should be titled 'Evidence-Based Policing' as the course curriculum is tailored to teach students about EBP; it is just disguised as 'Applied Criminology'. It has generated over 200 individual research projects from participants since 2013. The program is fulfilling the directive Weisburd and Neyroud made in their 2011 article, 'Police science: Toward a new paradigm', in which they urged police leadership to take an active role in the direction of police research, so that the police would be driving research agendas rather than academia. In the Cambridge program, this is exactly what police executives are doing.

The students at Cambridge are expected to produce a quality research project for their thesis. They are guided by an academic supervisor who assists them with understanding the field they are studying, developing a project that adds to the scientific literature, and designing the research, and it is then up to the student to implement the project in their police department. The Master's program lasts for two years, which gives the officers enough time to develop and implement field research. One project completed by Chief Tony Farrar of Rialto Police Department in California took the honour of being the first RCT of body-worn cameras (BWCs). This led to multiple other students engaging in studies on BWCs that eventually led to a multi-site study on BWCs. Many of these studies were published in academic articles, which speaks to the quality of studies the officers were turning out (Ariel et al, 2015, 2016; Drover and Ariel, 2015). The Cambridge Master's program is constructed to give support to an officer as they navigate implementing field research. The support is imperative. When anyone engages in learning something new, there will be failure and frustrations. What is needed is a supportive network of people who have been down that road, who can give advice on how to navigate some of the difficulties, help problem-solve when a challenge arises that no one has seen before, and in some cases, just be a good listener.

The Cambridge program is just one example of a formal degree program that focuses on EBP; there are many other Criminal Justice and Criminology programs throughout the world that, although they don't specifically teach EBP, support it. George Mason University offers both a Master's and PhD course in Criminology, and houses a Center for Evidence-Based Crime Policy. Drs David Weisburd and Cynthia Lum are two of the biggest proponents for EBP in the USA and they run the Center. Dr Lum has been involved in the development of The Matrix, a research-to-practice translation tool that the Center has on its website. It is a visual tool that organizes moderate to very rigorous evaluations for crime prevention based on the nature of the target, the extent to which the strategy is proactive or reactive, and the specificity of generality of the program (Lum et al, 2011). Many of the graduates of George Mason University's Criminology program have gone on to become applied researchers, assisting police departments with field research all over the world. Other universities that advocate for evidence-based practices that are in the USA are:

The University of Cincinnati, Temple University, Arizona State University, Texas State, San Marcos, and the University of Missouri, St Louis. The UK has the University of Cambridge and Canterbury Christchurch University, and the College of London has a Department of Security and Crime Science. In Australia, the University of Queensland and Griffith University both have robust evidence-based programs in Criminology, and in New Zealand, the University of Waikato is building up its crime science section of its Criminology program to accommodate the New Zealand Police's new Evidence-Based Policing Centre. A simple search of the colleges and universities in your local area may provide information on programs in that region that have an emphasis on EBP practices.

Building your own network

Building a network that supports your interest in EBP can be a critical step, especially for those working within institutional environments that may be less than fully supportive. A social network of individuals with a similar outlook and interests not only introduces you to new ideas, people, and experiences, but it is also relatively easy to do with the wealth of websites, messaging sites, and social media platforms currently available. And, as it happens, there is a growing body of research that shows the advantages of building such networks, from developing sounding boards for one's ideas (Drezner, 2017) to creating new collaborative opportunities (Grant, 2013) (for an extended discussion of the benefits of joining networks to foster change, see Coyle, 2017).

In the sections below, we again focus on providing some easy-to-use suggestions for building your own network. These steps include finding mentors, setting up group chats, attending conferences, and, of course, getting connected through the many groups that support research-based approaches to policing.

Societies

In his book *The Culture Code*, Daniel Coyle tells the story of innovator Tony Hsieh. When a consultant reached out to Hsieh for a meeting to learn more about one of his new projects, she received a two-line email followed by a list of names. The email simply said: 'Meet these people. Then ask them who else you should meet' (Coyle, 2017: 229). In a follow-up email, he offered only the comment: 'You'll figure it out' (Coyle, 2017: 229). As a result of reaching out to the people on the list, the consultant ended up not only with newfound knowledge, and a new network of likeminded people, but also a new job: as an executive member on Hsieh's project. Although Hsieh's advice is brilliant, you'll be happy to hear that our advice will not be nearly as cryptic. We think a good starting point for finding like-minded people is probably the easiest: follow Eric Barker's (2017) advice, and 'join a group'.

Joining a group with an interest in EBP has been made even easier thanks to the formation of the various Societies of Evidence-Based Policing. The first Society formed was the Society of Evidence Based Policing (SEBP) in the UK in 2010, closely followed by the Australia & New Zealand Society of Evidence Based Policing (ANZSEBP) in 2013, and then a few years later by the Canadian Society of Evidence-Based Policing (Can-SEBP) and the American Society of Evidence-Based Policing (ASEBP), both in 2015. Each of the Societies advocates for the use of research in police practice and mirrors the other Societies' aims: (1) increased use of best available research evidence to solve policing problems; (2) the production of new research evidence by police practitioners and researchers; and (3) communication of research evidence to police practitioners and the public.

The UK SEBP hosts an annual conference, featuring police officers and staff who have conducted interesting field research, as well as talks by leading academics from the field of EBP globally. They also support individual police services in the set-up of EBP by executive members, giving lectures and helping with the setting up of evidence-based hubs. Among the police services that have benefited from this assistance are the Staffordshire, Lancashire and Merseyside Police. Can-SEBP offers monthly newsletters, monthly webinars and podcasts, a series of easy-to-use research briefs (Square 1 assessments), a host of accessible research tools and tutorials in video, infographics and other formats, and weekly blogs on policing and policing research topics. ANZSEBP offers a reduced price to the *Journal of Experimental Criminology*, reduced conference prices, access to a forum dedicated to EBP, and to an online library of articles and conference presentations. ASEBP offers reduced conference fees to their annual EBP conference held every spring, access to bi-weekly research briefs on police-centered research, access to a bi-monthly newsletter, a discussion forum, monthly webinars hosted by Justice Clearinghouse, and a monthly blog (available at www.AmericanSEBP.org).

Social media

Connecting with people through the internet is an easy thing to do nowadays, especially with the onset of LinkedIn, Facebook, Twitter, and Instagram. Finding the academic or researcher who wrote on a specific topic is a relatively easy thing to do. Even if the academic is not on social media, most university professors give out their email addresses on the university's website and can be reached that way. Academics, like anyone, love to talk about their passion, so when contacted they will usually take the time to talk about their research and explain it in non-specialist terms. We have yet to see an academic ignore someone who is interested in their research – most academics want their research to be cited and used in the field. Many academics are on social media nowadays, and tweet about an article when it gets published. Following academics on Twitter who are researching your area of interest allows you to be notified when an article gets published. In a way, following policing scholars, practitioners, and others on social media creates your own, curated news feed. It helps you learn what is going on in the field and who is doing what types of research. Although it may seem that social media is more for beauty products, celebrity gossip, or fitness regimens, follow the right people and you will get your daily dose of EBP research.

In fact, there is an entire global EBP community available through Twitter. An excellent resource, for those in the UK and elsewhere, is a weekly Twitter chat known as #WeCops. Run by police practitioners, and guest hosted by people who are knowledgeable and passionate about the topics presented, #WeCops is an active discussion centered around three questions posed by the guest host. Topics range from police wellbeing, public health approaches to policing issues, police oversight, politics and the police, and even a few on EBP.

Another way to connect with leaders in the field is through LinkedIn (www.LinkedIn.com). This is a professional networking site that can be useful in connecting with researchers from around the world. Building a LinkedIn network is a necessity; even the EBP Societies have profiles on LinkedIn. Connecting to an EBP Society can open up an individual's network substantially. The people involved in police research understand that most of us are early adopters, thus they are usually very generous with their knowledge and time. They will help you connect to other people involved in EBP on LinkedIn or in other ways. Understanding EBP can be difficult and confusing; sometimes it may feel as though the research in policing is splintered and you aren't sure how it all fits together. Finding other people to help guide you through it is imperative, and LinkedIn can assist with finding the people you need to guide you. As you read books on EBP, listen to webinars, attend a session on EBP at a conference, or anything else you do to increase your knowledge of policing, you will make connections between all the information in the field. You will become familiar with the academics who study specific areas. And you will find mentors who are willing to share their time with you and teach you about EBP.

Mentors

As you begin developing knowledge, think about using one or two people as mentors to guide you. One of the authors has three mentors who have widely diverse approaches to police research. She has developed relationships with each of them to discuss different research methodologies, research projects, and life in general. She has three mentors because it averages out the dichotomy between their views on research; there is always a tie breaker between the two. Interestingly, research on successful executives has found that males tend to typically have two mentors and females three, with both groups reporting greater personal and work benefits than those without mentors (Roche, 1979).

You don't need to ask anyone to be your mentor formally. In fact, it's been suggested that you don't (Barker, 2017). You can develop a relationship by reaching out and asking simple questions about EBP or for advice. Mentoring relationships are built on whether you fit together. The relationship should be enjoyable for both sides, not just you alone. Eric Barker (2017: 215) has another cardinal rule we think should be observed: 'wasting a mentor's time is a mortal sin', so think twice before you hit enter. The example he uses is one that some of you may be familiar with: receiving a question that could easily be answered by Professor Google.

Mentoring isn't just one-sided. Try to bring something to the table when you build a mentoring relationship. If you are a student, you can give your opinion on what makes a class interesting or engaging. You may have read a paper that your mentor has not, tell them about the article, inform them of a piece of research they may have overlooked in the field. When you interact with your mentor, just make sure that every time you talk or email the need is not unidirectional. Make sure that occasionally you meet the needs of your mentor, whatever that may be. At a bare minimum, bring them a coffee at a conference when you see them to thank them for their time and energy.

Group chats

Maintaining relationships while working full time, studying full time, or doing both at the same time can be difficult. One way of maintaining your new networks and mentoring relationships can be through group chats. There are many apps for group texts that allow everyone to ask questions in a safe environment where they feel comfortable demonstrating their ignorance. WhatsApp allows for international group chats at no cost. This app was used to discuss the writing of this book, allowing us to share ideas, keep up to date on progress, and keep each other on track, even though we live in different countries – Canada, the USA and the UK. Technology has made us much more connected in some very helpful ways. Currently, one author is part of two separate group chats where people both talk about their personal accomplishments and ask police research-related questions. The group chat helps the group feel more at ease with each other, more willing to discuss the things they don't know and understand, and more willing to help each other. Group chats can be used before conferences to meet with people you have only met online. Your group can set a meeting time and place at a conference to catch up, learn, and exchange ideas.

Conferences

There are criminology conferences other than the SEBP conferences mentioned previously (see Figure 4.2). The two main criminology conferences in the USA are the American Society of Criminology (ASC) and the Academy of Criminal Justice Sciences (ACJS), in Europe the European Society of Criminology conference, the Eurocrim conference, the Stockholm Prize in Criminology conference, as well as a variety of others across the world. Conferences are a great place for networking, but do your homework first. Many of the top criminologists are busy people with packed conference schedules. Besides attending the conference, they are presenting, attending committee meetings, and meeting with graduate students and scholars they only see once a year at the conference. If you approach someone at a conference, make sure you arm yourself with a little bit of knowledge. Do not have the expectation that the connection you are trying to make is there to teach you everything. Ask them questions that you can only get from them alone and not from the internet or from reading their paper. Have some social awareness when approaching them, especially if this occurs after a presentation. They may have other people waiting to speak to them, so manage your time with them and don't take it all for yourself. This is a quick way to lose a good contact.

Attend the conference's social functions. Once again, before you go, arm yourself with a little knowledge. Look up people on the internet so you know who they are, read some of their research, or know what University or Research Institute they

Figure 4.2: An event at the Canterbury Centre for Policing Research

belong to. Have an opening line, 'Excuse me are you...? I read your article on ... and it made me think about....' Academics love to talk about their work, so talk about their work. Also talk about your work, especially if it fits within their area of expertise. Ask about their thoughts on your work, the methodology, the underlying theory, and your intervention, if there is one.

Making connections at conferences isn't as hard as you think. Everyone is interested in the same general topic as you are. If you are sitting next to someone at the hotel bar, just ask 'Are you having a good conference? Have you been to any good sessions? Any recommendations on which sessions to attend?' It's easy to strike up a conversation and meet people – you just have to be willing to put yourself out there.

The National Institute of Justice's Law Enforcement Advancing Data and Science (LEADS)

There are groups in existence other than the EBP Societies that are making efforts to bring like-minded scientific practitioners together. One of these groups is the National Institute of Justice's Law Enforcement Advancing Data and Science (LEADS) program that brings together practitioners from the USA and Canada (see Figure 4.3). The LEADS program was developed in partnership with the International Association of Chiefs of Police (IACP) to develop 'the research capacity of mid-career law enforcement personnel who are committed to advancing and integrating science into law enforcement policies and practice'. It was developed to shift the research paradigm from the view that only an academic can lead a high-quality research project to the view that well trained practitioners with a little oversight can conduct quality research. Individuals who have entered the program have rapidly picked up the tenets of

Figure 4.3: The National Institute of Justice's LEADS with Jim Bueermann (former President of the National Police Foundation) and Laura Huey (former Director of Can-SEBP)

EBP and begun to run their own RCTs. A LEADS from the Iowa Highway State Patrol ran a large state-wide hotspots RCT to determine if hotspots patrolling was an effective intervention for reducing vehicle crashes. He determined it was a successful intervention. Another LEADS from Vallejo Police Department in California partnered with BetaGov to run several rapid cycle RCTs (BetaGov was formed by a group of researchers from New York University to assist practitioners with running their own RCTs; see www.betagov.org). Another LEADS from Dayton Police Department in Ohio partnered with epidemiologists on reducing infant mortality and implemented a quasi-experiment testing home visitation by nurse volunteers. These LEADS projects and the hundreds produced by the Cambridge program demonstrate the ability of practitioners to understand and implement high-quality research in their own organizations. By creating a cadre of practitioners with these abilities, EBP might be able to reach a tipping point in policing that it has not been able to reach through academia and the federal funding of research alone.

Research partners

Finding an academic partner is probably one of the more difficult things to do. There is a dearth of policing researchers available in the field. If you have a local university with a Criminology or Criminal Justice program in your area, you can start there. If there is no such program, look at the professors who are in the Psychology or Sociology Department and see if any of them have an interest in delinquency, crime, or lifetime development. They might be interested in getting involved with a police department to conduct research. Attending conferences as previously suggested might also be a way to develop an academic partner. One of the authors, Renée, approached Dr David Weisburd about his work at the ASC conference. Renée developed this relationship and, over time, this led them to partner on the hotspots study she conducted at the Sacramento Police Department. Renée managed the project while being mentored by Dr Weisburd, Dr Cynthia Lum, and

Dr Chris Koper. In order to find a research partner, you have to take the first step to make a connection with a researcher.

Grants often require an academic partner to create a research design, forcing a police department into a relationship with a researcher. Finding a grant to partner on will help a researcher fulfill their obligations to their university or research institution. Working closely with the researcher, the practitioner can pick up the general concepts of what good research looks like. Many grants, like the Smart Policing Initiative grant through the Bureau of Justice Assistance (now the Policing Innovation grant) in the USA, have a support system set up through a training and technical assistance third party. In the USA, the technical training and assistance group is CAN, a consulting group dedicated to the advancement of science throughout the world. Grant participants are sent to intensive week-long training courses to build their understanding of research. The courses teach practitioners how to evaluate research against a rigorous standard, meet with other practitioners from across the nation, and sometimes meet their research partner in person for the first time. The ability to conduct high-quality research does not necessarily come from your background, but from a willingness to learn how to apply scientific concepts to the field.

Building the relationship over time and conducting more than one research project together rather than merely analysing a data set together allows both the researcher and the practitioner to accomplish their professional goals. The practitioner gets actionable information and the researcher gets data they can publish on. Take time to build the practitioner–researcher relationship, no matter which side you are on. Help them when they ask for assistance, especially when the ask is small, like introducing them to a potential partner. Your agency might not be able to partner on a project, but a neighbouring agency might. Renée has done this several times for different researchers. Her agency was not available to participate on several research studies, but she reached out to other agencies where she thought there may be an interest, and was able to connect the researcher with a willing agency. Just continue to build your relationships in any small way possible.

Summing up

We have reviewed several ways to learn about EBP as an individual in this chapter. Although the field of police research has been growing since the 1970s, the focus on EBP is relatively new, but the resources are growing: books, webinars, societies, and courses. There are many inexpensive ways to learn about EBP. There are many books that are starting to fill the stores, specifically on EBP. Start with one of the books previously mentioned to give you an overview of the field. As you grow your library, listen to the podcasts we mentioned, and participate in a webinar or two. Once you find your footing, start reaching out via social media and begin networking. Networking can cost you as little as your time or, at most, maybe a cup of coffee. Through your networking try to find an academic mentor who can focus your learning. Mentors can be found through networking or possibly one of the EBP Societies.

There are also academics at universities who are willing to help. Most of these relationships start out focusing on one problem, and through the exchange of knowledge, a relationship builds. Find the universities in your area that have a Criminology, Criminal Justice, Sociology, or Psychology program. There could be academics housed in those universities who are fascinated by policing issues and would love to assist with a research project. Reach out to researchers at large research institutes that conduct police research, such as RAND or RTI International. And don't forget the police officers who are ahead of you on this path. They can be exceptional mentors. Google their name from the research article you are reading, and then find their agency work email online or find them on social media. We constantly field emails from all over the world and try to respond to everyone who asks for help. Most of the people working in the EBP field are very passionate about their work so they are usually willing to help others. If you reach out to one, they can help connect you to others.

Conferences and classes can be financially prohibitive, so try to find conferences that are close to your hometown with inexpensive registration. The conferences held by SEBP, ASEBP, and ANZSEBP highlight the work by practitioners and academics. Australia, New Zealand, and UK police services host masterclasses on EBP conducted by some of the top academics in the field. For those masterclasses that require tuition, you might be able to fund the cost of a class through your agency or your university as professional development.

Take the first step in building your EBP knowledge. Being evidence-based feels difficult because it requires a person to digest an entire field of research and then to figure out how to best apply it in practice. Thankfully, the breadth of research in policing is still very narrow, so choosing an area to focus on is not as overwhelming as it first seems. To date, we have not met anyone who starts practicing evidence-based approaches who feels like they have it all figured out. At the beginning, everyone feels overwhelmed. Every journey starts with a first step. The best approach is to just take the first step, then another, and another. The next thing you know you are practicing evidence-based policing.

5

The smaller agency

Academic researchers have recently focused much-needed attention on the question of police openness or willingness ('receptivity') to adopt evidence-based approaches (Telep and Lum, 2014; Telep, 2017; Blaskovits et al, 2018). Of equal importance, however, is the question of how agencies can go about moving from intention to action, by actually identifying and utilizing the resources necessary to implement evidence-based practices. While some scholars (Lum and Koper, 2017; Ratcliffe, 2018a) and groups (the various Societies of Evidence-Based Policing) have tried to fill this void with practical suggestions, police practitioners – particularly those in smaller organizations – can be left feeling totally adrift in what is often entirely unchartered territory. We are not alone in observing the gap between receptivity and action: in a study of evidence-based training at the College of Policing in the UK, Fleming and Wingrove (2017: 205) found that whereas attendees held favourable views on the course content, they 'expressed concerns about the resources needed to implement evidence based approaches in their agency.' Further, participants felt 'the organizational structures and resources required to implement EBP were not currently in place' and were somewhat sceptical about whether organizational culture could change sufficiently to truly embrace the EBP ethos (Fleming and Wingrove, 2017: 202).

Fortunately, we are not advocating for wholesale change here, but rather, providing suggestions for how to effect smaller, incremental steps towards becoming more evidence-based in organizational decision-making. A starting point to that process is to recognize where any agency is at in terms of resources, but also cultural norms and openness to change. In this chapter, our focus is on what many might perceive to be the biggest challenge in implementing EBP: the 'small agency'. Throughout the pages that follow, we explore not only the limitations of smaller agencies, but also their strengths. We provide insights, experiences, and research-based ideas and suggestions for developing evidence-based practices within services that may typically have fewer resources on which to call. Recognizing this fact, we tell smaller agencies how to make the most with the resources they have and, where possible, how to find additional resources and support. We also identify various stumbling blocks and limitations that smaller agencies may face and, where we can, offer potential solutions.

The smaller agency

For our purposes, a small agency is one in which there are fewer than 100 sworn officers. Whereas agencies of this size might not be the norm in the UK, Australia, and some other countries, in much of the USA and parts of Canada it is not unusual to find agencies of this size. In fact, law enforcement surveys in the USA reveal that about half of all local police services employ fewer than 10 full-time officers (Reaves, 2015). In both countries, smaller agencies are typically the result of the desire for local control of police services by towns and communities. Indeed, in Ontario, Canada, where Laura lives, the alternative to taxpayers funding a local police service is joining with another municipal agency to create a regional service or contracting policing services from the provincial police agency. While many communities see contract services as satisfying their needs, and enter into contract arrangements with larger service providers, there are still thousands of smaller agencies within North America alone.

Contrary to the old adage 'bigger is better', when it comes to implementing evidence-based policing (EBP), this is not always the case. In fact, another adage might be more apt: '"mo" money, "mo" problems'. What do we mean? It's been our experience that, because of the flatter hierarchical structure, smaller agencies are sometimes able to adopt, adapt, and innovate more quickly and creatively than larger organizations. As there isn't often a large budget with which to draw on to support large-scale projects from places like New York or Los Angeles, smaller agencies are less likely to engage in 'naive policy transfer' by simply borrowing ideas from other services with the expectation it will work. Instead, you tend to see much more local innovation, some of which we will describe below.

All of the above does not mean, however, that there are not significant challenges to implementing EBP within smaller agencies. Resource issues are a main challenge. Simply put, it can be difficult for individuals within agencies to find time to break away from other duties to engage in developing and testing new programs. Someone still has to be out on the road, responding to calls. A great example was recently provided to us when we attempted to implement EBP in an agency with about 80 sworn members. Our original plan was to host a two-day workshop on EBP that would provide not only relevant training on EBP basics and concepts, but also help the organization to create a blueprint for implementing and sustaining change. Our plans quickly went awry when confronted with a dose of reality. The reality check came in the form of a response by the sergeant organizing the project on behalf of his service. As he noted, trying to incorporate individuals from all sections and divisions of their agency for a two-day workshop presents a logistical nightmare. He explained, "this would require overtime, scheduling, and operational backfill." The plan was quickly amended based on his suggestions – one of many examples where police experience and knowledge can be critical to program success. Also, one of many examples where size matters.

Starting from scratch: identifying resources

Here's some good news: every organization, agency, institution, or group of any size likely has people with a level of investigative skill, field knowledge, critical reasoning, curiosity, problem-solving abilities, initiative, and the other personal qualities that are helpful for understanding, using, and even creating research. In fact, unless your police service excludes university or college graduates from recruiting pools, you probably also have one or more individuals with at least some training in locating and reading research and in the basics of research methodology. What we want to do in this section is to help smaller agencies to identify resources and begin to maximize their potential to grow EBP within their service.

Early adopters

In order to grow any innovation, it's important to have at least a basic understanding of how ideas catch on. Long before anyone ever used the internet-speak of 'going viral', Professor of Communication Studies, Everett Rogers (1962, 2010), had charted the processes by which new ideas are increasingly adopted over time to reach a critical mass. Called the 'Diffusion of Innovations' theory, Rogers (2010) argued that diffusion occurs as a result of five factors: (1) innovation; (2) communication channels; (3) time; (4) social system; and (5) adopters. Of these, we are the most interested in adopters, and in particular, early adopters.

Who are early adopters? When it comes to helping to spread innovations within or across organizations, early adopters are of special importance to the process. These are the individuals and groups who today would be referred to as 'influencers' or 'thought leaders', because they combine a high social status within their organization that is based, in part, on a reputation for being discerning, and thus highly selective, when it comes to adopting cutting-edge innovations. They don't innovate those new ideas, and nor are they the first to use them (those are 'innovators') (Rogers, 1962, 2010). However, they form an important, if small, group of users that makes those new technologies, programs, philosophies, and so on, of interest to broader audiences.

In the EBP world, many early adopters tend to be those individuals we call 'pracademics', those police practitioners and civilian police employees who combine first-hand knowledge and experience with some understanding and use of research methods. To be clear: early adopters are not exclusively pracademics or people who might see themselves as falling within that category. We introduced you to Chief Andrew Fletcher in an earlier chapter. He was not only an early adopter for his police service – commissioning several research projects and sitting in on discussions of methodology and how to implement research – but he was also instrumental in helping to promote EBP to other police services across Canada. This is an example of someone who is an early adopter and an active influencer within a small-sized agency. And no, you don't need to be a chief to wield this kind of influence within an agency; we have seen several examples of sergeants, staff-sergeants, inspectors in the UK, Canada, and elsewhere, who are also influential early adopters.

Aside from commissioning studies, there are some other activities that an eager early adopter can undertake to increase adoption within their own agency. Fortunately for us, in an article on how to champion EBP, Sherman and Murray (2015: 9) proposed several different strategies, none of which are limited to agencies of any particular size: inspire fellow police professionals to get better results from better decisions; connect a network of fellow professionals who produce and apply evidence; identify the need to make any decision with better results; suggest ways of gathering or analysing the need for a decision; defend against the use of entirely intuitive decision-making; uphold the integrity of research evidence, no matter how inconvenient the results; and praise the work of colleagues who apply to improve police practice.

One of the most important things that police services interested in EBP can do is to recognize and support their early adopters. Again, size should not matter here. One of the smallest agencies we work with is running a complex study off the desk of one of their community engagement officers. Why? Because he showed the value of not only the work itself to the organization, but also the value of the enhanced research training he would receive, training they recognized would benefit future projects.

Captain Jason Potts,
Vallejo Police Department,
California, USA

Working in a small agency, I have found that introducing EBP concepts in small doses and having one-on-one conversations with officers of all ranks to be invaluable. Explaining *why* we are testing an intervention is important to the frontline officers. In small agencies, resources are not plentiful, so care must be taken to use them wisely. I discovered that it is just as important to prove something does not work as it is to show that it does. This way of thinking tends to resonate with cops as they see a potential purpose for testing – not just testing for the sake of it or implementing a program for perceived self-serving reasons.

Crime analysts

When used to their full potential – that is, as gatherers and analysts rather than solely as producers of basic crime stats – crime analysts can be one of the single biggest assets to a police department looking to implement EBP (Piza and Feng, 2017). We are not alone in this assessment; others have similarly observed that 'crime analysis is essential to the effective deployment of the strongest evidence based policing strategies such as POP [policy-oriented policing], hotspots policing, and focused deterrence, in actual practice' (Smith et al, 2018: 304). And, given the fact that many departments hire crime analysts, post-PhD, with significant graduate-level training in social scientific research methods, some police services have staff members who are fully capable and willing to conduct complex empirical research, including RCTs and longitudinal studies. That said, one of the challenges that many smaller agencies face is a budget that does not stretch towards hiring a full-time crime analyst and/or being able to free up an analyst's time in order to allow them to conduct research beyond their ordinary duties.

Given the challenge stated above, what options are available to the smaller agency? One agency we work with is in this boat: they do not have a crime analyst on staff, making any type of in-house research a daunting task. For this agency, which wanted to run an RCT on a new school program, Laura was able to provide external research support in the form of an interested researcher located about two hours away. The researcher agreed to work with BetaGov and the police chief in developing the methodology, collecting and analysing the data, with the agency running the trial and thus producing the data. In the case of another smaller agency, which employs only one analyst, the challenges were twofold. First, because this individual was the only one to produce the department's statistics and other research, freeing up her time to run a complex research project would be a hardship. Second, because so much of her time is spent on operational tasks, she did not have the skill set to engage in the methodology this study required. In this instance, they were able to secure the services of a doctoral student to work with the analyst in collecting the data. Additional analytical support was provided by an analyst with more experience in this technique at another agency. This type of cooperation between agencies is not only helpful but can also lead to cross-agency collaborations that benefit both services.

Data and data tools

The contributions that operational policing data have made to the field of Criminology, and to the development of innovative policing research in particular, are innumerable. To briefly illustrate, police data have been used to evaluate the effectiveness of police interventions in relation to crime hotspots (Groff et al, 2015; Sherman and Weisburd, 1995), problem-oriented policing strategies (Braga and Schnell, 2013), foot patrols (Ratcliffe et al, 2011; Andresen and Malleson, 2014), and focused deterrence strategies (Corsaro et al, 2012), as well as to identify spatial dimensions of criminal offending (Townsley et al, 2000; Bowers and Johnson, 2005; Ratcliffe and Rengert, 2008), the size and scope of criminal networks (Hashimi et al,

2016), and the characteristics of traffic accidents and fatalities (Brubacher et al, 2014), among other important public safety concerns. Quality data from police agencies can increase the overall volume of empirical research on policing and community safety issues, providing policy-makers and police leaders with an improved base on which to draw when making important policy decisions. It can also help to identify and track internal changes in relation to employee safety, wellness, and other administrative issues (Cordner, 2018). In short, the importance of quality operational and other policing data for police analysts, researchers, program evaluators, and others cannot be understated (Brimicombe, 2016).

Unfortunately, there can be significant problems in how police data is collected and verified. For example, a study one of us attempted on the utility of using foot patrols to address crime hotspots failed due to significant coding errors in police occurrence reports. An attempt to analyse Canadian missing persons data at the national registry was confounded by the fact that there is no reporting requirement for solved cases. In another study, the idea to use police-generated statistics on 'time spent' in relation to a policing activity had to be abandoned when it was realized there were no standards in place as to how 'time spent' was defined, rendering the statistics produced meaningless. To be clear, while data error is hardly unique to smaller agencies, it can be compounded in smaller agencies due to a lack of personnel to ensure verification protocols are followed, overworked frontline supervisors with too little time to ensure reports are filed correctly, and/or having no crime analysts to clean 'dirty' data.

Leaving aside, for now, the problem of 'dirty data', what can smaller agencies do to use internal data to conduct quantitative and qualitative research beyond producing basic crime and other stats? The answer is quite a lot, and surprisingly, much of this work can be done affordably, efficiently, and without advanced training. How so? Through the use of a wealth of research tools and instructional resources that are readily available. Regardless of the specific software used, most police records management systems (RMS) used allow for searches and data dumps of both summary and detail records into Excel spreadsheet files. Once in Excel, data can be analysed directly (both quantitatively and qualitatively) in the Excel program or otherwise imported for use by such programs as:

- NVivo (qualitative coding and analysis software)
- Stata (software for running different types of statistical analyses)
- ArcGIS (software for creating geographical-based analysis)
- R (stats software)
- SPSS (stats software).

Most of these same programs have free download demo versions to try out, can be leased to individuals for fairly reasonable costs, provide instructional materials, and/or have generated a raft of 'how to' videos on YouTube. For more information on resources for practitioners, see Chapter 9.

Creating more resources

One of the single biggest mistakes an agency can make is to put all of their EBP eggs in one basket, so to speak. Examples of this type of error include having an 'EBP expert' and/or limiting evidence-based initiatives and decision-making to one unit or group of individuals. Why is that a mistake? As we know from other types of initially successful initiatives in the policing world (see Skubak Tillyer et al, 2012), strategies that are largely or wholly dependent on one or more key players risk failure if and when those individuals move to other roles or agencies. In Chapter 8 we discuss how to create longer-term sustainability through management philosophies and practices; however, before we get there, a good intermediary step is to create more resources beyond those identified in the previous section. Thus, the goal of this section is to provide some methods for creating new and more internal resources.

In-service training

In theory, EBP sounds fairly self-explanatory: the police should base decisions on research. However, as we've explained, it's a bit more complicated than this. Again, it embodies not one idea (research is good), but five equally important principles. We'll save you the time and trouble of flipping back a few pages and simply re-present them here:

1. Scientific research has a role to play in developing effective and efficient policing programs.
2. Research produced must meet standards of methodological rigor *and* be useful to policing.
3. Results should be easily translatable into everyday police practice and policy.
4. Research should be the outcome of a blending of police experience with academic research skills.
5. Policing issues should be addressed through careful targeting, testing, and tracking of implemented solutions.

Our own research (Huey et al, 2018a), as well as studies conducted by our colleagues (Telep and Somers, 2017), suggests that a deeper knowledge of, or familiarity with, these principles can often be missing from practitioners' understanding of EBP. This is not at all surprising given that exposure to EBP, as well as to research principles and methodology more generally, is going to vary across individuals (Telep and Somers, 2017). To truly grasp not only the concept of EBP and its foundational principles, but also such necessary considerations as 'what works?', 'what doesn't work?', 'how to evaluate whether something has a base', 'rigor', 'targeting, testing, and tracking', among others, we have found it useful to offer in-service training for interested police services. The benefit of such training is not only that it provides fundamental knowledge for the beginner, but it can also serve as an opportunity for would-be pracademics to present their ideas, receive feedback, and in some instances, begin the process of realizing those ideas through the development of a research project.

While this all sounds great in theory, as noted earlier, it can be challenging to provide such in-service training within a smaller police service. Ideally, you would want it offered through every rank and position within an organization, particularly as your future leaders will be drawn from across those ranks; however, a 'total system's approach' is not likely to be feasible for an agency of fewer than 100 sworn officers, which is also having to deal with staffing difficulties around mandated as well as other 'non-essential' training. Even a bare-bones introductory course will take an officer off the road for a period of three to four hours, never mind anything approaching hands-on or experiential learning. A further challenge is that many smaller services are located in more rural or remote areas. Even if they were able to schedule in-service training from an outside expert, costs may be prohibitive. What to do?

One approach is to focus training on individuals in higher ranks and have them 'push down' EBP definitions, knowledge, tools, and other information to those under their supervision (Telep and Somers, 2017). Another strategy, and one that is being developed, is to make EBP knowledge and tools widely available through online training, knowledge sources, and tools. The impetus behind this strategy is to ensure equal access to officers and civilian staff regardless of their location or agency size. We provide information on how these resources can be accessed in Chapter 9.

Experiential learning

In trying to promote the uptake of EBP-based learning, various groups across the globe have developed 'bespoke' workshops (Fleming and Wingrove, 2017) and 'masterclasses' (Brown et al, 2018) aimed at exposing police practitioners to EBP principles, introducing expert researchers, and presenting some of the new and more cutting-edge work with which the police can engage. These types of courses have high value, particularly for those just getting started. However, offering such training – as noted above – is not always practicable, and requires further efforts to help practitioners bridge the chasm between concept and use. Thus, when it comes to learning about research, we ascribe to the maxim that, as in most things, 'experience is the best teacher'. As a result, whenever it's feasible for an agency to do so, we advocate for adopting hands-on learning that allows individuals to directly acquire knowledge and skills through trial and error, and to do so when their operational or administrative duties permit.

Again, larger agencies may seem to have some advantages when it comes to permitting staff to develop and test their own research. For example, a larger agency may be more flexible in allocating time away from other duties or providing shift or other coverage. A larger agency can also typically provide a greater degree of analytical support, including assistance with research design and data extraction. That said, with the new range of products and services available for free, or at low cost, it *is* possible for the smaller agency to also get involved in hands-on learning through conducting their own research. One recent example is neatly provided by a sergeant in a 75-member service, who combines his community engagement activities with research into crime prevention. Partnering up with BetaGov, he was able to rely on their research expertise and oversight to help him develop the project, execute the research, analyse the results, and prepare the findings. The project? A test of a public education initiative aimed at reducing theft from autos (TFA). First, they identified their TFA hotspots and, with help from BetaGov, randomized locations so they could be set up TFA areas as either an intervention or control site. Next, residents within the intervention sites were mailed crime prevention messaging on postcards from the service. In short, with the approval and support of his organization, and training and guidance from outside academic researchers, this small agency was able to successfully conduct an RCT, which would be a daunting task for many experienced researchers, never mind a novice.

Building a library

A common complaint in the world of EBP is the inability of potential consumers of research to access peer-reviewed work behind paywalls – that is, published work that is only accessible to subscribers or those willing to pay a download fee. Before presenting some possible solutions to getting access to quality research, let's briefly explain academic publishing and why much of it is subscription-based. Like policing, academic performance is measured based on a set of ostensibly objective (that is, number of tickets handed out) and subjective (that is, making a 'good arrest') criteria. In academia, key indicators of a strong academic career include publishing (in top journals), research grants, research awards and honours, and graduate supervision. These journals are typically edited by academic editorial teams on a voluntary basis, but professionally managed by publishing houses, which ensure print runs, manage copyediting, lay out articles and volumes, advertise, and so on, and that costs money. To offset publishing costs, researchers can opt to make their work 'open access', but will be charged, on average, between US$2,000 to US$4,000 per article. Where possible, researchers can budget for these funds from research grants, but for those with smaller funding pots, the difference between having an article as open access or not could be the difference in funding a graduate student.

Now, although there are online, open access journals available, we urge caution in using them. They are often a place of 'last resort' for articles that could not get published in higher-quality, print journals. Some are even 'predatory', open access journals that exist solely to make a profit from a researcher's inability to publish elsewhere due to poor data, poor methodology, and/ or terrible writing. Anyone who has been in academia for any period of time has quickly found themselves inundated with requests to publish in unrelated and/or obscure journals that promise to process your paper in a very short period of time, for a fee.

How to get around all of this and still get access to decent quality research? We have a few tried and true suggestions. The easiest: check your local library. In doing research into what information could be freely accessible to police services in Canada, we quickly discovered that many Canadian public libraries provide access to academic databases for library patrons. All that was required was a local library card.

If you are possibly among those who do not have public library access, there is still hope. One suggestion is to use RSS feeds on journal websites. What is this? RSS is web-based feed that provides users with updates to online content. For example, if you subscribed to the RSS feed of the journal *Policing & Society*, every time the journal updates its content with new papers, you can be informed. Some of these papers will be subscription or pay only, but you can also see which ones of interest, if any, are open access (free to download and use). Another strategy is to subscribe to free online journals and newsletters put out by reputable groups. A great example of this is the magazine *Translational Criminology*, produced by the Center for Evidence-Based Crime Policy at George Mason University in the US. Similarly, the Australia & New Zealand Society of Evidence Based Policing (ANZSEBP) publishes *Police Science*, a free bi-annual journal available in both print and online to members (and membership is free).

Books are also a great source of information on research, but can be quite costly. And, if space is an issue, they can also take up a fair amount of room. One strategy that has been employed by the Canadian Society of Evidence-Based Policing (Can-SEBP) is to purchase a communal eReader (a Kindle) and to set it up with a sharable Amazon account.

Incorporating a little, some, or a lot of evidence-based policing

In our ideal world, every police service across the globe would be fully committed to an evidence-based approach at all levels of the organization. We are, however, pragmatists, and so we recognize this is probably never going to happen. It won't happen for a variety of reasons, including, but not limited to, finances, resources, internal politics, external politics, and the need for immediate responses in unknown situations. Thus, our focus here is on offering some basic ways in which the small agency can incorporate a level of EBP that is compatible with the agency's goals, and that is comfortable for where the agency is currently at in terms of their orientation towards evidence-based decision-making. This is not to say that at some point in the future the level of engagement with EBP and/or the desire to become more evidence-based will not change. It might. But for now, we advise you to go at your own pace and to see which, if any, of our suggestions might work. And while we're at it, let's start off with a little primer to help you get started (see Figure 5.1).

Figure 5.1: Beginner's guide

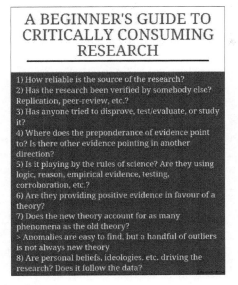

Source: Ferguson (2019)

Systematic literature reviews

Without a doubt the simplest and most effective way to become more evidence-based is to evaluate how your agency accesses and uses existing research. What do we mean by this? It's been our experience that, when police services do turn to the relevant research literature, the current standard for most is a bit haphazard. As a result, police leaders are asked to make decisions based on what can sometimes be a poor evaluation of the available knowledge. Here are some common mistakes we have seen over and over again:

- 'Cherry picking' the literature, that is, only selecting those studies that fit a pre-determined conclusion.
- Limiting the search to what is easily found on Google or another common search engine.
- Not carefully assessing the quality of the studies or reports used.

- Failing to set up other criteria for what will be included or excluded.
- Not providing a complete overview of all of the relevant studies consulted.

What's the alternative, you ask? The systematic review (SR). Simply put, the SR is a technique for 'finding, sifting, sorting and synthesizing the findings of primary evaluations relevant to particular interventions' (Johnson et al, 2015: 460). To do this, the researcher creates a set of questions to be answered by the research literature and then sets out a comprehensive plan for searching for relevant papers. Identifying beforehand what will be included and excluded from the search results should, in theory, reduce some of the biases we find in 'cherry-picked' literature reviews (Uman, 2011). In practice, an SR could look like Table 5.1.

Table 5.1 is intended as just a guideline and not the definitive statement on what you should or should not do. Clearly, your SR will be shaped in large part by what your research questions are and/or the type of literature you may have available. One of us (Laura) was once taken to task by an academic researcher for proposing something similar because it didn't include what is termed 'grey literature.' Grey literature includes documents, evaluations, and other types of material that have been produced by governments, the private sector, academics, and others, that typically have not been subjected to academic (or any) peer review. Although it is plentiful in Google search results, we do not usually recommend relying on grey literature because the quality of much of it produced in the policing world is substandard. There, we said it.

Although we do not have the space to provide a comprehensive overview of the different ways in which someone could conduct an SR, we will present a brief description of three types we find suitable for police services seeking to better understand the relevant literature (see Table 5.2).

We have some good news for those of you who might be slightly panicked at this point. Systematic scoping and narrative reviews are fairly easy to do. Meta-analysis is clearly more

Table 5.1: Systematic review steps

Step	Activity	Example
1	Identify research question(s)	What forms of in-service training on diversity issues have been evaluated by researchers (by topic)?
		What forms of in-service training on diversity issues have been shown to be effective in changing officer attitudes?
2	Set up a search strategy	Where will you search? (eg, academic databases)
		How will you search? (eg, using a university search engine)
		What keywords will you use? (eg, police, training, diversity)
3	Establish inclusion criteria (what sources will you include?)	Must be a peer-reviewed study
		Must be based on an experiment
4	Establish exclusion criteria (what sources will you exclude?)	Paper did not describe research methods in detail
		Study was not published in English
5	Coding	I will count how many studies I found
		I will tag/colour code/highlight every paper according to the topic of the training
		I will tag/colour code/highlight every paper where the authors reported a positive or negative change in officer attitudes

Source: Authors' own

complex and requires a significantly more advanced skill set. The good news is that nobody is asking you to become a master statistician. All you need to know is that, when it comes to program evaluation and the question of 'what works', being able to point to the results of *someone else's* meta-analysis and say, 'this is the strongest we currently have available' is all you would need to be able to do. The even better news is that there are many sources of free, easy to read, downloadable meta-analyses on which you can easily draw. Again, we have identified a few of these in Chapter 9!

Table 5.2: Systematic review types

Scoping review	A type of review in which all of the research in a given area is identified, including by content and research methodology
	For example, trying to map the overall volume and content of Australian publications of policing research
	Findings for this type of review can be presented both numerically (number of studies found on a topic) and in narrative form (description of the overall findings in an area), although usually more emphasis is placed on numerical results
	It is useful for when researchers are working with quantitative, qualitative and mixed-methods studies
Narrative review	Findings for this type of review are presented in narrative form, with the author describing and interpreting their results
	For example, describing the overall content of articles on focused deterrence as a strategy
	Narrative review is a particularly helpful approach for when researchers are reviewing studies that are primarily qualitative
Meta-analysis	This is a form of review that uses statistical techniques to pool the effects of multiple experiments to assess whether – overall – there is reason to believe that a program worked
	For example, assessing the strength of hotspots policing as a policing strategy by combining statistical findings across multiple studies
	Findings are presented numerically, often in the form of a 'forest plot' that maps out individual findings relative to other findings

Source: Authors' own

Program evaluation

Beyond the literature search, the most basic form of EBP is the program evaluation. Ideally, any new program or policy would be evaluated to see whether it meets its creator's stated goals and objectives (Cordner, 2018). The most common version of an evaluation in policing uses a pre- or post-test design in which someone:

- Creates a baseline measurement of X (X being whatever the phenomenon is the policy or program is meant to impact).
- Introduces the policy or program.
- Re-measures X to see if the policy or program had any impact.

There are, of course, other ways in which to conduct a program evaluation. The above design typically relies on statistics that an agency is already collecting, whether that be operational or administrative data. That said, where there is no pre-existing data, testers can create baseline and post hoc measurements using surveys, questionnaires, or other similar approaches. We have also conducted program assessments for which survey data alone would not provide enough information to get a more accurate sense of how a program is functioning. In such instances, qualitative interviews with key personnel may also be appropriate.

Regardless of where an agency is in terms of its commitment to becoming evidence-based, many do some form of program evaluation, and all agencies should aspire to assessing both new and current initiatives. We would also argue that the more rigorous the evaluation, the better the data. Better data means decision-makers receive a more accurate picture of just how well their programs and policies are actually doing.

When it comes to measuring program effects, not only should no program be immune from assessment; we would argue that this includes how well an agency is doing in terms of becoming evidence-based. This is something we have done ourselves with some of the smaller and mid-sized agencies we are working with to implement EBP. Using a pre- or post-test design, we have been measuring changes in officer and staff attitudes and behaviours with respect to becoming more evidence-based. There are any number of existing studies from which an agency or researchers could borrow relevant sample questions. For ourselves, we have used both a modified version of the Telep–Lum (2014) receptivity questionnaire (Blaskovits et al, 2018), and one designed by Gary Cordner as part of his work with the National Institute of Justice's Law Enforcement Advancing Data and Science (LEADS) project.

Experiments

If you were a little bit daunted over the thought of doing a program evaluation, we can see how the thought of conducting experiments within your smaller agency might seem like an impossible task. The good news is that not only is this entirely possible, but we can also recommend some resources to assist you, as well as providing suggestions to help you get started.

To begin, we need to introduce you to three key concepts with which all police agencies should have some degree of familiarity. These are Sherman's (2013) 'triple-Ts', which should be the basis of any experiment within policing:

- *Targeting:* the identification of a high-priority policing problem (that is, a place, crime pattern, type of offense).
- *Testing:* implementation of a strategy to fix the problem, which is simultaneously tested through rigorous scientific research to ensure the strategy had the desired effect (such as crime reduction, increased arrests, improvement in community satisfaction).
- *Tracking:* once in place, a solution should be tracked over time to ensure it continues to work as desired. If not, adjustments should be made, and evaluated and tracked over time (Huey et al, 2017: 545).

Research and observation suggest that most agencies have little problem with targeting problems to be addressed (see Sherman, 2013; Neyroud, 2015; Huey et al, 2017). Where things tend to fall apart is with testing. While many agencies do test interventions − new strategies, new policies, new techniques − they may use inappropriate measures, inappropriate methodology, and/or fail to set appropriate goals and objectives for evaluating success. Where things really go off the rails is with tracking. As police services tend to rely on simple pre- or post-test measures to analyse success or failure, there is often a lack of willingness to revisit 'successful' strategies to see if they are continuing to work after the experimental period (Neyroud, 2015). Why would a successful strategy stop working? For a variety of reasons, including personnel changes, loss of funding, resource issues, and demographic shifts in targeted communities, among other factors. In short, if you're going to engage in experimenting new techniques, be sure to commit to both a short- and long-term assessment process.

While it is beyond the scope of this book to provide you with detailed instructions on how to conduct different types of experiments, we can refer you to several available online resources to help you get started (see Chapter 9). Further, we can also recommend the services of groups like BetaGov, which exist to provide research support to police and other criminal justice agencies across the globe.

Summing up

In this chapter, we have focused on smaller agencies and how they can adopt an evidence-based approach, by highlighting some of the advantages and challenges they may face. We demonstrated how the flatter hierarchical structures of small agencies could enable more rapid diffusion of innovation and new ideas, while also pointing out how the lack of human and other resources can become a limiting factor.

To aid smaller agencies and the people within them in maximizing benefits and addressing limitations, we provided some practical suggestions based on empirical research and police practice to enable the growth of EBP among small agencies. For example, identifying early adopters of EBP to act as change champions can help garner support for the initiative throughout the agency. Similarly, crime analysts can and should play an important role in embedding EBP through their collaboration with external researchers and other agencies in acquiring knowledge regarding innovative practices. Small agencies can also utilize available resources such as their records management systems (RMS) more effectively by conducting analyses on available data in software that is available free or at a reasonable cost. To avoid dependency on a single EBP expert, agencies can create an awareness of EBP across the organization through strategically managing available opportunities. This can be achieved through in-service training of a top few who will then disseminate the information to others in the organization. Making use of free online training tools, experiential learning through hands-on research, accessing resources through public libraries and free online resources, systematic literature reviews, program evaluations, and conducting experiments can also be useful for a small agency in the implementation of EBP.

6

The mid-sized agency

While it might seem that mid-sized agencies typically have greater resources than smaller services, this doesn't mean they always know where those resources are, or how to best make use of them when it comes to implementing evidence-based policing (EBP). This reality is often reflected in the fact that many larger police services, despite having trained research staff, pracademics, and/or other resources to hand, do not appropriately target problems or test or track new initiatives (Slothower et al, 2015). To illustrate: a recent survey on receptivity EBP approaches by mid-sized Canadian police services found 'mixed views were expressed by respondents in relation to their agency's ability to target high priority policing problems and to test strategies for fixing these problems ... [and] views were overwhelmingly negative when respondents reflected on how well they thought their agencies track the effectiveness of strategies over time' (Huey et al, 2017: 544).

In this chapter, we focus on identifying existing and potential resources that mid-sized agencies can draw on to implement EBP practices and maximize research creation and use. We also present successful strategies and practices that have been used by police agencies across the globe, and discuss the strengths and limitations of those approaches given resource, workload, funding, and other issues. We explain where challenges might lie for the mid-sized agency, as well as some ideas for surmounting obstacles. And, as in other chapters, we draw on the relevant literature, our own experiences, and the experiences of police officers who are working within the EBP domain, to present some old and some new ideas for implementing different EBP strategies.

The mid-sized agency

We have defined as a 'medium' or 'mid-sized' agency one in which there are 100 or more sworn officers but fewer than 1,000 (100–999). As is the case with smaller agencies, police services in Australia and the UK will generally not meet this criterion.[1] By way of contrast, it has been estimated that there are some 700 'mid-size' agencies in the USA alone (IACP, 2014). In the USA and Canada, mid-sized agencies are typically municipal or smaller regional or county services. We can point to Akron Police Department in Ohio (approximately 450 officers) as an example of a municipal service and Camden County Police Department in New Jersey (approximately 400 officers).

In relation to strengths, although there are more levels of hierarchy and thus more layers of bureaucracy in a mid-sized agency than is found among their smaller counterparts, mid-sized agencies can be surprisingly nimble and flexible when it comes to adopting new ideas and practices. And, as we discuss in greater detail throughout this chapter, having more police officers and more staff can sometimes translate into greater resources to call on, and more freedom for employees to engage in EBP.

To be clear, not all mid-sized agencies have the ability – some might say the relative luxury – to be able to task senior staff with engaging in research to improve organizational efficiencies. At a similarly sized municipal service in another part of the same country (about 240 sworn members), an inspector reacted with discernible frustration to the idea of embedding EBP. Citing the possibility of staffing cuts, a growing workload, and increasing operational burdens as barriers to taking on any new tasks or ideas, he simply – and understandably – saw any new mode of policing as being something that could not be taken on when he and other staff were struggling with staying afloat. In this case, and in similar others, it's important to remind people that EBP does not have to be about taking on immediate, wholesale change. In fact, we'd never advocate for that perspective, as it would likely be doomed to failure. As this inspector and others were told, take on what you can, no matter how small, and do it when you can.

Starting from scratch: identifying resources

In this section we examine how mid-sized agencies can begin to marshal internal resources towards the goal of increasing their uptake of research and other EBP goals.

Early adopters

As within smaller agencies, mid-sized services seeking to embed EBP can benefit greatly from those individuals who recognize the utility of EBP and support EBP initiatives from their early stages. The advantage many mid-sized agencies enjoy is a more diverse pool of potential key influencers within and across the organization. These may be individuals who are already engaged in supervisory, evaluative, and/or research-related roles and thus have some familiarity with evidence-based decision-making (Magnusson, 2018), or they may include those who are new to policing research but who are highly regarded within their services and who are recognized and valued for being forward thinking.

One of our favourite examples of an early adopter is an officer, who, as a staff-sergeant, became an early EBP champion within his mid-sized agency. Rather than seeing engaging with research as an activity that should be done by others, he dived right into the deep end. With the goal of better understanding the research process and how to generate actionable research, he paired up with BetaGov to conduct his own RCT. Further, being blessed with a highly supportive chief, he also championed an external hotspots study to help his agency enhance knowledge of how their crime hotspots had formed and how to effectively police them through a combination of focused patrol and other strategies. As early adopters tend to do, the more he learned, and the higher the enthusiasm he generated, the more he shared his positive experiences and views of EBP throughout his organization, including inviting external researchers to discuss EBP and EBP initiatives at his agency's annual planning meeting. Through his actions, this early adopter made research a much more palatable commodity within his organization and, because of his rank, showed that EBP does not necessarily have to be a top-down process, but one that can be championed by anyone with sufficient social capital within an organization.

To be clear, however, it's not all happy stories. Over the years, we have seen a number of early adopters who sought to embed EBP and/or otherwise generate institutional change fail to initiate any level of buy-in from their agencies. There are some common factors that underlie these failures. One is an institutional preference for the status quo. There's an old saying, 'the only thing cops hate more than change is things staying the same'. Often this has to do with how the nature of the change is described. Is it presented as continuous change that will enhance current practices? Or is it perceived as a type of discontinuous change that will require behavioural and/or attitudinal changes that might not be seen as particularly desirable (more work, new policies, additional training, more supervision)? While early adopters may readily embrace change, most potential adopters are simply looking for an improvement to existing operations, that is easily understood and employed (Moore, 2014). Having faced more than one stressed police manager, we are aware that many are not inclined to gravitate towards tackling new intellectual challenges, additional complex puzzles, or worse yet, a crash course in research methods. This is why any attempt to move EBP beyond an agency's early adopters has to include a strategic plan for bridging the gap between an early adopter and those who may jump onboard if they perceive the conditions to be right (Moore, 2014). Again, this means constructing a version of EBP and/or EBP strategies that:

- Serve a *useful* purpose within the organization.
- Can be done in a manner that is *understandable* to anyone.
- Are *easy to use* from an administrative and operational standpoint.

Deputy Chief Colin Watson,
Victoria Police Department,
Canada

You require an EBP champion – someone with a passion for doing better, who is willing to challenge the 'normal' way of doing business, a person who can influence others, who can organize a movement, is strategic in their approach, and patient in the process. You cannot be discouraged when at first you don't have everyone jump on board and get it – it won't happen. However, you must be persistent, look for easier 'wins' early, and build off the small successes. Don't approach it like a program; seek to change the culture – that takes time.

Another factor that can derail the ability of an early adopter to effectively promote EBP is a relative lack of social capital. The reality is that individuals who are perceived as pushing new ideas without holding sufficient status within an organization tend to be marginalized, if not punished, within groups. As Adam Grant (2016: 65), neatly explains,

> Power involves exercising control or authority over others; status is being respected and admired. In an experiment led by University of North Carolina professor Alison Fragale, people were punished for trying to exercise power without status. When people sought to exert influence but lacked respect, others perceived them as difficult, coercive, and self-serving. Since they haven't earned our admiration, we don't feel they have the right to tell us what to do, and we push back.

This is something we have seen first-hand. Individuals occupying a low status within their organizations, who are full of excitement and enthusiasm, have seen their efforts at promoting EBP and other new ideas come to nothing. In most instances blame is laid at the door of the inherent conservativism of policing. That is, however, only part of the equation. In two notable instances we've been told by several others within the same organization that the problem wasn't the idea; it was the person promoting it. What we've learned from our own experience, and from research by Fragale, Overbeck and Neale (2011), is that successful early adopters have to have sufficient influence to not only achieve buy-in from their leaders, but also from their peers. So, for those struggling with this in their own departments, it may be worthwhile taking a page from Adam Grant's (2016) *Originals* and to try to find those influencers in your own service who might offer some political support and a willingness to run with your ideas.

Crime analysts

In contrast to smaller agencies, which may not have a full-time crime analyst, it has been our collective experience that most mid-sized agencies have at least one, if not more, individuals conducting crime and/or patrol analysis. Beyond the basics of crime analysis, crime analysts are typically engaged in preparing reports on crime statistics, deployment patterns, and calls for service, as well as identifying crime and disorder patterns or trends. Less frequently, they may also be involved in program evaluation activities, including developing, implementing, and testing new policing and crime prevention strategies (Piza and Feng, 2017). Unfortunately, as we note, along with our colleagues Weisburd and Neyroud (2011) and Santos (2014), more often crime analysts remain a largely untapped resource within police agencies, their skills, knowledge, and talents limited to producing basic statistical analyses on Excel spreadsheets, cleaning data, trying to answer questions for which that data was never collected, or identifying potential targets for new strategies.

Those agencies that *do* provide opportunities for crime analysts to actively engage in research can find themselves fostering new and creative responses to traditional policing problems.

To illustrate how valuable crime analysts can be to the process of developing in-house innovations, we turn to the example provided by, Sheri Bell, a crime analyst in the Winnipeg Police Service in Canada. In 2017, Sheri was inducted into the Center for Evidence-Based Crime Policy's Hall of Fame for not one, but two, initiatives. The first was the Smart Policing Initiative. This program combined place-based, deterrence-focused, and problem-solving strategies across the City of Winnipeg. As the project lead for the testing component of the study, she guided a team that implemented a mixed methodological evaluation that drew on both police and community survey data. In Laura's letter of nomination, she wrote,

> ... this is one of the first major, indeed most ambitious studies, of targeted policing activities in Canada and was undertaken with little academic support. This was Sheri's initiative and, drawing on her own self-taught understanding of evidence based policing, she pushed her Service to understand not only the importance of testing the initial intervention, but also tracking it over time.

The second project for which Sheri was recognized involved a Crime Prevention through Social Development Initiative ('Gerry's Kids'), which sought to identify young people with a history of offences, and have officers work with young people to reduce the effects of previous negative or adverse contacts. 'Gerry's Kids' became an official project when the police officer who had informally initiated positive contacts with runaway youth sought Sheri out to find out how he could evaluate what effects, if any, his work was having. Sheri then developed a comparative analysis that tracked key indicators – arrest and other data – to determine if program outcomes were being met (namely, changes in young people's attitudes and behaviour).

The point we are trying to make here is simple: crime analysts can be significantly important actors in implementing EBP – that is, if your organization actually utilizes their services to their fullest capacity (Keay and Kirby, 2018).

Data and data tools

The mid-sized police service is not always immune to data problems. In research conducted by Huey and Koziarski (in review) on data issues within police agencies, they found that, although the mid-sized agencies studied had greater resources for ensuring clean data – including verification and audit personnel – problems in coding still ensue. That said, larger agencies, by dint of sheer size, can be treasure troves of data for potential projects. For example, one service's missing persons data alone, extracted from their records management system (RMS) into a basic Excel spreadsheet, generated something in the nature of four different projects.

It's important to keep in mind that police services also produce a wealth of administrative data that can be helpful for constructing research into personnel and other related issues. Among other potentially impactful topics there are likely to be data available internally on recruitment and retention issues and employee wellness. And, perhaps most importantly, the people within the organization are often the best experts on a given topic, and conducting interviews or surveys can provide huge benefits to an organization. Returning to the example of the missing persons project undertaken by one mid-sized agency, one piece of the overall puzzle entailed conducting exploratory interviews with Search and Rescue personnel, detectives, and frontline officers to explore both 'what works' as well as the challenges they face. Those interviews yielded critical information on the risk assessment tool they were using, and the fact that it had become out of date due to demographic shifts.

While the mid-sized service may benefit from access to more software tools to analyse data, a wealth of free or low-cost packages are also available. We strongly urge you to investigate what is out there and to perform a basic assessment as to which might be beneficial, given needs and context. To illustrate how useful this exercise can be, one of the agencies with whom we work wanted to identify a set of risk factors from their case data. While they could have used Excel, we suggested they try NVivo, a qualitative software package that is useful for coding keywords and identifying themes within interviews and other kinds of data. Our goal was simply to introduce them to another tool that could be used to meet not only current but also future needs. The principal propelling this advice was Maslow's (1966) famous saying: 'if all you have is a hammer, everything looks like a nail'. Although Excel might have worked fine in this instance, why not take the opportunity to trial something else that might provide greater functionality for future analyses?

Creating more resources

Having identified some preliminary resources and tools on which mid-sized agencies can draw to get started on their EBP journey, we want to turn our attention to an important issue: creating an even greater number of resources in the form of personnel who can effectively commission, synthesize, use, and generate research, as well as providing the means of accessing the tools and technologies on which they can rely. After all, if we are to ensure the survivability of any new initiative – and this includes efforts aimed at implementing EBP – then increasing internal capacity is a paramount concern. In the following, we provide some ideas as to how mid-sized agencies can effectively and efficiently take on this task.

Basic evidence-based policing training

In our experience, many mid-sized agencies have already adopted – whether consciously or not – programs and strategies that fall under what we would consider to be the umbrella of EBP. Does this make them EBP agencies? We would argue, not necessarily. Why? Because it's one thing to adopt a practice like hotspots policing, but it's another thing to have everyone within your organization understand why you're doing it, especially those tasked with ensuring the success of that strategy. One of the problems we consistently find in relation to implementing EBP is that knowledge of EBP, where it does exist, remains the property of a few people within an organization, and thus 'for many police agencies and their leaders, the rhetoric of being evidence based far outstrips the reality' (Martin and Mazerolle, 2016: 35). This point was brought home to one of us during an EBP training workshop with a mid-sized agency that was already using a hotspot-based approach to their patrol work. During the course of a group discussion, a frontline sergeant admitted, in somewhat frustrated tones, that he didn't actually understand the hotspots approach and why the patrols were being directed as they were. In response, an equally frustrated inspector replied that he had sent out a memo by email. Hadn't the sergeant read it? The lesson learned: if the success of your policing initiative relies on people reading and understanding emailed memos, you might have a problem.

Although memos might seem an easy and quick method for sharing vital information, when it comes to implementing EBP, we strongly advocate for something that might stand a better chance of ensuring content is understood and taken up: training. In the previous chapter, we discussed EBP training as a useful starting point for creating internal resources within a small agency. We also see this as necessary for mid-sized agencies; however, in this chapter, given the personnel advantage that many mid-sized services enjoy relative to their smaller counterparts, we are taking a slightly different approach. In this section we briefly discuss introductory EBP training as a form of 'basic training' that can be built on through successive education and training initiatives aimed at developing specific skills among personnel. As the latter is really about generating sustainable EBP efforts, we discuss this in a later chapter. For now, our focus remains on introducing EBP.

As with both smaller and larger services, we highly recommend that any agency about to embark on adopting and implementing EBP begins by exposing their people to training that includes a significant review of the principles of scientific reasoning, research methods, the central tenets of EBP, as well as some relevant examples of 'what works', 'what doesn't work', and 'what might work' based on the policing research evidence base. How to deliver this training?

- *Internally taught courses.* Whereas smaller agencies might lack the capacity to craft their own in-service training, many, if not most, mid-sized services have training staff. Because a central tenet of EBP is knowledge sharing, trainers without a background in the area are fortunate in that there is a sizeable volume of information, resources, tools, and even training modules, publicly available to draw on in developing their own courses. And to make things even easier, we have created a guide to help readers locate credible resources you can access (see Chapter 9).

- *Bringing in experts.* A number of individuals, groups, and organizations are willing to conduct in-house training on EBP and EBP-related topics. Some organizations offer such training for free; other individuals and groups charge a daily rate.

- *Externally taught courses.* As EBP catches on, we have noticed an increase in the number of colleges and universities offering courses and programs that include some or a lot of EBP content. For some agencies, funding registration in existing college and university programs might be a worthwhile idea. And, if an agency already has a pre-existing relationship with a local higher education institution, they might also want to consider exploring co-developing such courses.

- *Expert seminars.* Occasionally, some experts in policing research or related fields do offer instructional seminars and workshops. The EBP Twitterverse is a good source for finding out when and where such events might be occurring.

Experiential learning

Before undertaking several projects to embed EBP in Canada, Laura and Hina (along with other researchers) conducted a series of survey and interview-based studies to examine the extent to which Canadian police agencies were 'receptive' to EBP (Huey et al, 2017; Blaskovits et al, 2018). One of those studies, based on interviews with police leaders from across Canada, directly explored the extent to which police leaders were not only open to EBP, but also understood what it was, and felt confident in their abilities to make decisions based on research evidence (Huey et al, 2018b). What we found should not be surprising: despite the fact that few had graduate-level training in research methodology, every single police leader stated they felt equipped to make evidence-based decisions (Huey et al, 2018b). Our own experience in working in the trenches alongside many police leaders, frontline supervisors, and others is that any confidence expressed early on in the research process quickly disappears quickly when it's time to actually execute a study or conduct a systematic assessment of the extant literature. Our own analysis of this situation in Canada revealed that most leadership and supervisory training courses – the staple of advanced in-service training – either do not adequately prepare future leaders for evidence-based decision-making or do not touch on research matters at all (Huey et al, 2018b). Only those who had done advanced degrees in research-intensive universities had any of the skills necessary, or the knowledge to know what they didn't actually know about research (Huey et al, 2018b). Our experience in other countries suggests this finding is not unique.

This isn't to say that you need to have a graduate degree to understand and use research; many of the savviest creators and consumers of research are police leaders with high school degrees. What they have in common, however, is an interest in learning and working with new ideas and ways of thinking. They're the ones who never miss a research meeting and are among the first to ask questions (including those dreaded questions that begin with 'I'm not sure I fully get this ...'). What they don't do is silo research or rely on others to do the heavy lifting. In fact, we would hazard a guess that one of the biggest mistakes an agency can make is to dismiss the importance of direct experience and knowledge of how research is created and can be used when it comes to evidence-based decision-making. A prime example of how this happens is when police leaders silo research within one particular unit or limit research functions to one individual within an organization, who then gets tasked with providing analysis with recommendations. What this does is:

- Limit the potential for leaders, supervisors, and other decision-makers to develop a solid grasp on what is and what is not good empirical evidence in support of a policy.
- Force leaders and other decision-makers to be largely, if not completely, dependent on others' assessments of that evidence.

- Provide decision-makers with an easy 'out' for not engaging with research at all, if they don't like the recommendations.

What to do ensure that decision-makers understand how to use research to make decisions? As in the previous chapter, we encourage mid-sized agencies to take on experiential learning projects — that is, to have interested employees try their hand at producing research. There are probably many, many ways in which to do this, but two primary ways in which this has successfully been done in the past are:

- Having staff members generate mini-research proposals to be subjected to a review. Successful proposals can then be developed internally under the guidance of the crime analysis unit or program evaluation personnel (where appropriate).
- Having staff members work under the guidance of an external expert who has the necessary knowledge and skills to supervise research.

As it happens, we have an example:

Victoria's SVU (Special Victims Unit) analysis

The Victoria Police Department (VicPD) in British Columbia, Canada, took an entirely different approach to experiential learning. They teamed with a researcher (Laura) and held two one-day EBP workshops, which led to the creation of an EBP working group. Drawing on an idea from one of their inspectors, one of VicPD's deputy chiefs drew up an application for grant funding to develop a research project analysing the growing complexity of sexual assault investigations. The plan? To use a mixed-methods approach to comparatively analyse cases from 2007 and 2017 to better understand what factors may be impacting changes in investigational work. The working group then built on their methodology by identifying the specific factors (variables) to be analysed and, following half-day training on NVivo software, utilized their new training by analysing the collected data.

Building a library

Any agency seeking to start down the EBP path should consider creating a reference and resource library that will be accessible to all police personnel and staff. Fortunately, we have laid out several low-cost options in the previous chapter for smaller police services, and each of these options is also readily available to the mid-sized agency.

An option more readily available to mid-sized and larger services is the ability to also create a data library. What is this? It's a computer (or computers) hosting various software and data sets (such as stats on call volumes, calls for service types, GIS [geographical] data, and so on) that staff could use to learn, practice, or employ their data analysis skills for projects of interest. Why a data library when you have crime analysts? Multiple reasons come to mind, including the ability to create new skills and knowledge among personnel, as well as reducing workload strains on busy crime analysts. A data library could also be set up in such a way that it also provides crime analysts with opportunities to hone skills and learn new programs and techniques. In short, it creates a physical space for sworn members and staff to become creative in understanding and using data, as well as understanding data limitations and challenges.

Incorporating a little, some, or a lot of evidence-based policing

In this section we explore some of the ways in which mid-sized services can begin, or advance, their use of EBP. Again, this is not meant to be an exhaustive list for those seeking total organizational immersion into using, creating, and/or actioning research. We recognize that interest in engaging with EBP is varied, and thus we are not recommending turning everyone within a department into an 'evidence cop' (Sherman, 2015) with a burning desire to run multi-site studies. In some cases, an agency may be content with having some internal research expertise in the form of in-house researchers, whereas another may find it 'good enough' to have 'evidence informed practitioner[s] armed with basic knowledge of where to find relevant research, how to apply and integrate with other resources, together with the tools to engage in some basic evaluation' (Brown et al, 2018: 124). Therefore, our suggestions below offer some ideas for different types of mid-sized police services.

Systematic literature reviews

As we've discussed previously, systematic reviews are a great – and more rigorous – method than simple literature reviews for developing an enhanced understanding of the research literature. And fortunately, many of the tips and tricks we've outlined for smaller services will also apply to mid-sized agencies. However, one area where a mid-sized agency may have an advantage is in being able to schedule outside training on how to conduct systematic, scoping, and meta-analysis reviews. While many, if not most, police services may not have long-standing relations with academic partners who can come and conduct research training for a day, it is the case that most have a local college or university within driving distance. Simply putting in a query to their administrative staff or professors could net new and interesting collaborations.

Program evaluation

It might be easy to think that program evaluation is both a routine function of many agencies, and one that tends to be well done. In our experience, neither is the case.

What are some of the more consistent problems we see?

- *Data quality issues.* Inaccuracies in coding and verification can run evaluations aground.
- *Data that is not fit for purpose.* Data is often collected within agencies for one purpose and then expected to be magically useful for other purposes, most of which were not intended when the data was collected.
- *Lack of pre-planned objectives and goals.* Many programs we encounter lack well-defined objectives, so it can be difficult to measure possible success when criteria for success are judged against retrofitted goals.

- *Poor implementation.* Many programs are implemented with little concern for 'fidelity', that is, by ensuring that people actually do what they are expected to do. It is difficult to measure program effects when necessary actions are not being taken.
- *Fudging.* No program creator wants their 'masterpiece' to fail, which can place a strain on evaluators to suddenly come up with the 'right answer' to the question 'does this work?' One thing we have seen time and time again is program evaluations in which methodological corners are cut, and data sources announced in the methods section suddenly go missing from the analysis, with the end result being that a rosy picture of success emerges. While this finding may be satisfying to the program creator, it can create a false picture of whether institutional resources are being employed effectively and efficiently. EBP practitioners believe that there is an ethical imperative to know 'what works' (Mitchell and Lewis, 2017).

As program evaluation is a cornerstone of EBP – letting practitioners know what is and is not truly working – cleaning up the problems identified above is imperative.

Experiments

The growth of EBP internationally has ushered in a new and exciting phenomenon: a commensurate growth in the number of mid-sized agencies now conducting experiments, both on their own (using internal resources) and/or in collaboration with external partners. What makes this development so exciting is:

- It shows that experiments and/or more complex forms of research *are* entirely do-able outside of larger agencies.
- Each study conducted has the potential to help build the evidence base in a given area (so the more, the better).
- Studies conducted by smaller and mid-sized agencies help EBP practitioners better understand not only 'what works',

but also under what conditions different programs, policies, and practices succeed or fail.

While providing technical instructions on how to conduct experiments is outside the scope of this book, there are plenty of free resources available on everything from research design to data coding and analysis. Chapter 9 will provide you with loads of reference materials to help you get started or to up your research game. In the meantime, what we'd like to focus on here is highlighting some of the innovative experiments conducted by mid-sized police services to help identify various project ideas, methodological possibilities, and so on, for those readers potentially interested in conducting research and wondering what can be done given resources and other issues facing mid-sized services.

In Table 6.1 we've compiled a short list of some experiments undertaken or currently underway by mid-sized agencies across the globe that might be worth considering as potential projects for you or for your organization.

Canada

The Durham Regional Police Service (DRPS), in collaboration with Lakehead University, conducted an experiment alongside Toronto's Festive RIDE line (a check post for intoxicated driving) to test the potential benefits of body-worn cameras (BWCs) (Saulnier, 2019). During the experiment, the officers wore BWCs for eight shifts and did not wear them for the remaining seven. Officers made a 10-second introduction at the stop, and those wearing BWCs also informed the motorists of the presence of the camera and recording taking place. A survey was conducted to gauge citizens' experiences at the RIDE line, and whether a BWC made a difference in the officer–citizen interaction. The results revealed that a BWC positively impacted police–public interaction as well as public perception of the police in general.

Like many cities and towns, London in Ontario, Canada, has a problem with bicycle thefts. The problem is particularly acute in two sites: the city's downtown core and on the university

Table 6.1: Experiments

	Size (sworn)	Experiment
Police service, Canada		
Durham Regional Police Service (Ontario)	850	RCT – body-worn cameras
London Police Service (Ontario)	650	Pre- or post-test – crime prevention messaging
Barrie Police Service (Ontario)	218	RCT – situation tables for high-risk individuals
Halifax Regional Police (Nova Scotia)	615	Systematic observation – verbal de-escalation
Police service, USA		
Arlington Police Department (Texas)	361	RCT – body worn cameras
Tempe Police Department (Arizona)	327	RCT – de-escalation training study
Fayetteville Police Department (North Carolina)	425	RCT – police training study
Spokane Police Department (Washington)	310	RCT – body worn cameras
Madison Police Department (Wisconsin)	479	RCT – hotspot patrol study
Riley County Police Department (Kansas)	107	RCT – hotspot patrol study
Vallejo Police Department (California)	109	RCT – automated license plate reader technology
Iowa State Patrol	370	RCT – hotspot patrol and community policing study
Police service, UK		
City of London Police	756	Mass deployment of TASERs

Note: RCT is short for randomized controlled trial, a Level 5 experiment on the Maryland Scientific Methods Scale (SMS).

Source: Authors' own

campus. Having seen some experiments in reducing similar thefts in the UK, they decided to replicate a visible deterrence study. To do this, they identified bicycle stands in both locations and randomly placed giant posters featuring a pair of eyes and the message 'We are watching you'. What they found was a very modest reduction in bicycle thefts and a new appreciation for the challenges of running experiments in the real world. Unlike the laboratory, where processes can be more carefully controlled, things don't always go to plan with policing experiments. One key consideration is making sure frontline officers are aware of expectations placed on them (see Ratcliffe and Sorg, 2017), as well as the importance of recording data accurately. With the London bicycle study, crime analysts ran into difficulties because of the second issue: there were problems with recording the locations from which the bicycles were taken.

The beauty of this exercise isn't that it produced ground-breaking results or singlehandedly solved the bicycle theft problem in London in Ontario, Canada; it's that it provided the service with an opportunity to experiment with crime reduction strategies in a controlled fashion, thus allowing members to learn about how to undertake similar innovative projects in the future. Just because a program doesn't achieve major results doesn't mean it wasn't valuable to the organization.

Barrie Police Service is working on a one-year RCT evaluating the 'Collaborate Barrie' situation table. This multi-agency project helps mitigate the escalation of risk to individuals identified as being potentially vulnerable, enabling optimal utilization of resources. Individuals are randomly assigned to the situation table while the control group receives a routine response. This is an ongoing initiative, and the RCT will follow the subjects for an additional six months to determine the effectiveness of the program.

An evaluation by the Halifax Regional Police utilized systematic observations of officers in videotaped simulations, comparing a baseline group of officers to officers trained in Verbal Judo (see Chapter 9) (Giacomantonio et al, 2019). Overall, the study found that five simpler behaviours (such as identifying oneself or providing a reason for contact) of the 15 coded behaviours encouraged by the training were impacted at a statistically significant level. However, more complex behaviours (such as empathizing with the subject) were not impacted. The evaluation also found that the likelihood of utilizing de-escalation skills decreased as an officer's years of experience increased.

United States

Arlington Police Department (APD), in collaboration with the Police Executive Research Forum (PERF), conducted an RCT to assess changes in citizen perceptions due to BWC use (Goodison and Wilson, 2017). It was expected that as a result of BWC use there would be (1) fewer citizen complaints; (2) voluntary involvement with the police would generate a positive perception of the police; and (3) interactions with officers wearing BWCs would lead to stronger perceptions of police legitimacy. A total of 84 volunteers were trained to use BWCs and were randomly selected during each shift to use the cameras. The researchers obtained data from APD on citizen complaints for the entire city during the pilot period as well as for the same six months one year prior to the study. Results suggested that officers who were trained in BWCs during the study experienced a 38 percent drop in complaints between the year prior to the pilot study and the same six months a year later, during the pilot study. During this time, all other APD officers experienced a 4.1 percent increase in citizen complaints. Overall, respondents had favourable impressions of their interactions with APD police officers.

Tempe Police Department's Smart Policing Initiative has developed a violence de-escalation training program based on the expertise of the top de-escalators in the department, identified by their peers (White and Pooley, 2018). Focus groups with the top de-escalators have further identified principles of de-escalation based on BWC footage. The effectiveness of the training program will be tested using an RCT experiment in which half of the officers assigned to the treatment group will receive de-escalation training whereas those in the treatment group will not. Behaviours among the two groups will be compared using surveys of officers, citizens, use of force, and complaint data, and BWC footage. The Smart Policing Initiative team will test whether the de-escalation training led to significant changes in officer behaviour resulting in fewer complaints, use of force, and improvement in citizens' perceptions of the police.

A training evaluation involved a partnership with Fayetteville Police Department (FPD) and Tucson Police Department (TPD)

(Wolfe et al, 2020). The evaluation was focused on determining whether tact, tactics, and trust (T3) influenced officers' attitudes and behaviours regarding social interactions, and whether the amount of training influenced these outcomes. A protocol was developed in collaboration with each police agency whereby a high-dose condition received six months of T3 training, and a low-dose group received three months of training. All patrol officers were either assigned to experimental training or control conditions using rosters within each agency, and an RCT was used to evaluate T3. A post-training questionnaire was administered at each agency to gauge officer reactions to both the content of the training and the design of the program. Results suggested that T3 is successful in modifying a trainee's attitudes towards certain practices of procedural justice.

Spokane Police Department (SPD) tested the effectiveness of BWCs issued to all patrol officers using an RCT design (Wallace et al, 2018). Officers were randomly assigned to either treatment or control using a random number generator. The BWCs were assigned on a rolling schedule as groups of officers were trained on consecutive Fridays during the two deployment months. Computer-aided dispatch (CAD) data were also utilized that only included calls answered by the officers in the study. Results of the study showed no evidence of statistically significant passivity in officer behaviour due to camera use, while self-initiated calls increased for officers assigned to treatment during the RCT.

To address rising gun violence, Madison Police Department started the Violence Reduction Initiative that focuses on resources and crime reduction in hotspots identified by their Criminal Intelligence Section (Mosiman, 2018). Since the program is based on engagement and enforcement, extra resources were allocated to the hotspots, including community walking patrols 10 to 15 minutes several times a day for engaging with residents and law enforcement through arrests. The evaluation results for the West District suggest a 66 percent reduction in shootings and 72 percent reduction in violent crimes. Another positive outcome was officer job satisfaction that increased significantly due to positive feedback from residents.

Riley County Police Department (2020) started the Laser Point Initiative to reduce crime by focusing on smaller hotspots for very short periods. Crime analysts select new hotspots each week and the officers assigned focus on issues such as crime and traffic problems. Preliminary results are encouraging, and indicate reductions in both crime and calls for service in the targeted hotspots.

A study by Vallejo Police Department involved randomizing patrol cars equipped with automatic license plate reader (ALPR) technology to help with theft detection (Potts, 2018). Officers selected cars based on seniority and were blinded to the study condition. The vehicles in the experimental group had the ALPR alert function on while those under the control condition had their alerts off. Results showed that police cars equipped with ALPR technology showed a 140 percent greater ability to detect stolen cars. Fixed ALPR (stationary units) were found to be more efficient than mobile ALPR in making arrests, as officers tended to sit downstream of fixed locations waiting for hits, resulting in more custody arrests. The control data also showed that 35 percent of all hits were misreads for the mobile readers, with a similar number (37 percent) for the fixed readers.

The Iowa State Patrol and George Mason University's Center for Evidence-Based Crime Policy developed a proactive and problem-oriented strategy to enhance public perception of law enforcement presence and to reduce traffic accidents (Clary, 2019). Troopers make 10- to 20-minute visits to each hotspot for crashes and engage in highly visible citizen interactions at bars, gas (petrol) stations, and convenience stores. The purpose of these visits is to ensure the safety of patrons and to convey safety messages through direct interactions and leaving behind literature on traffic safety. Results suggest that traffic fatalities have fallen since the implementation of this strategy, and work is underway to collect more detailed performance measures for a longitudinal evaluation of the intervention.

United Kingdom

The City of London Police studied the effect of mass deployment of TASERs on policing (Ariel et al, 2019). Eighty-four frontline response officers received training on technical and behavioural knowledge required to use TASERs in field operations. TASER-equipped officers were assigned to treatment clusters while officers without TASERS were assigned to control clusters. The findings showed that the presence of a TASER was related to a 48 percent higher incidence of use of force during treatment conditions for TASER-equipped officers, a 19 percent higher incidence for non-TASER equipped officers, and a 23 percent higher rate force wide compared to control conditions. The assaults of officers doubled, indicating that the presence of TASERs leads to increased aggression, and both enhanced training as well as concealment of TASERS should be considered to prevent such incidents.

Summing up

The focus of this chapter has been on how mid-sized agencies can, in many respects, be in a much better position to adopt evidence-based approaches compared to smaller and larger agencies. This view is based on the fact that mid-sized agencies tend to have higher levels of resources than smaller services, and fewer levels of hierarchy than their larger counterparts.

Drawing on successful strategies used by the police globally, we suggest measures that these agencies could adopt, given their resource and operational constraints. Mid-sized agencies have a larger pool of individuals familiar with evidence-based decision-making, who can influence others to adopt these practices. This can be achieved through the development of strategies that are useful, understandable, and easy to use, by utilizing the skills of crime analysts in the agency and making use of administrative data that can be helpful for constructing research into personnel and other related issues. To enhance the internal capacity for innovation, we recommend that police agencies invest in basic EBP training through internally taught courses, expert knowledge, externally taught courses, expert seminars, and experiential learning. Developing an in-house data library, conducting systematic literature reviews, program evaluations, and designing experiments would also help mid-sized agencies understand the conditions under which different programs and policies work.

7

The larger agency

Throughout the early part of the 2010s, the City of New York, and New York Police Department (NYPD) in particular, were generating significant positive attention over the fact that the city's crime rate had dropped at about twice the national rate (Roeder et al, 2015). Heralded as the 'New York Miracle', commentators observed how the City that had formerly stood as a symbol for crime, social disorder, and urban decay was now the City that had become 'safe' (Zimring, 2013). Some have credited NYPD's use of Wilson and Kelling's (1982) 'broken windows' approach as generating declines in certain offences (Sengupta and Jantzen, 2018); others cite police use of the CompStat model to target district-level offences as the primary catalyst of change (Zimring, 2013). Regardless of what actually drove New York's crime decline, cities across the globe began to look to New York as offering potential solutions to adopt in response to their own local conditions.

That New York became a site from which other, frequently smaller, police services sought to poach crime fighting ideas is not surprising in one sense: larger police services often have the financial and human resources to develop and test their own innovations and/or to trial new technologies. To illustrate: the first major trial of body-worn cameras (BWCs) in the UK was with Devon and Cornwall Police, and the Toronto Police Service were the site of the first trial in Canada, both agencies with more than a couple of thousand sworn officers. Similarly, we find two other major municipal agencies – Los Angeles and

Dallas – as two early adopters of predictive policing software. While larger agencies can clearly lead the way in trialling new innovations, we have to be careful not to draw too many conclusions from this. Access to significant resources – relative to other police services – does not automatically translate into a greater degree of innovation or an increased willingness to embrace change. Indeed, change in larger organizations can be long, slow, and difficult.

In the pages that follow, we argue the importance of laying a solid foundation for creating cultural change within larger police services. This can be done, we suggest, through identifying existing internal resources, as well as by creating new ones. Larger agencies, while sometimes better resourced, face greater encumbrances when trying to get their employees behind an idea, so we also consider strategies for motivating internal stakeholders. Further, we provide examples throughout the chapter of what incorporating evidence-based policing (EBP) in a larger agency can look like. Additionally, we examine the obstacles larger agencies may face when attempting to generate change.

The larger agency

As may be recalled from the Introduction, we categorized any police service in which there are over 1,000 sworn officers as a 'larger agency'. This may seem a bit unusual given the size of organizations such as NYPD (approximately 32,000 sworn members) or the London Metropolitan Police (approximately 31,000 sworn officers); however, in many countries that have neither regional nor federal policing services, or that do not have major metropolitan areas of the size and scale of Chicago or Los Angeles, 1,000+ officers *is* a larger police service.

While all police organizations have hierarchical structures, navigating these to create cultural change can become significantly more difficult within larger organizations. Simply put, larger organizations have a greater number of levels, each with its own decision-makers, and thus, potentially, a more diverse pool of opinions across those levels as to what progress should look like and how it should be achieved. Not surprisingly, institutional bureaucracy often stifles innovation (Dyer and Dyer, 1965; Thompson, 1965), and this is no less the case in policing (Willis et al, 2007. Our own experience of promoting evidence-based innovation within larger police services supports this view: with each layer of approval required, the number of discussions, reports, and other materials required to get problem-solving and evidence-based tactics off the ground increases exponentially, frequently wearing down the most dedicated of potential innovators.

Given the difficulties we have identified above, the question becomes: how do you go about transforming the institutional mindset of a larger organization? The answer: the organization must go through a process before it realizes the benefits of its investment in EBP. Progress is slow, but nevertheless there will be long-term gains as well as quick turnaround wins. These wins are as a result of developing people to be critical thinkers in the way they approach problems. To become a critical thinking police agency, you must first create a culture of curiosity, where the people who work there ask themselves, 'is this the best way to do things, and how can we do it better?'

Starting from scratch: identifying resources

In this section we take a slightly different approach from earlier chapters. One of the biggest obstacles facing proponents of change within larger agencies tends to be institutional culture rather than access to resources. Thus, the first step to implementing EBP within the larger agency should be an honest assessment of an agency's organizational culture and its overall willingness to embrace change.

Appetite for evidence-based policing

It is nearly impossible to drive change within an organization that does not desire it, and where its people are incapable of objectively observing flaws in current operations. For a police agency to adopt an evidence-based approach, there must be a general willingness to operate in an evidence-based way.

While this may seem obvious to most readers, in practice there is often a large disconnect between what people say they desire – to be more evidence-based – and how they act – such as implementing untested programs based on individual experience or group intuition. We have seen this many times over in large agencies – a strong desire to be evidence-based – but when faced with the reality of the hard work it takes to learn and understand EBP practices and to overcome cultural resistance, the desire quickly wanes. Another issue in large agencies is the inability to make rapid changes. In one US agency, EBP training was conducted for executive management, but by the time the organization developed the internal capability to execute EBP practices, the majority of the executive management had been promoted to other organizations or retired, requiring a whole new iteration of EBP training for the new commanders.

In those cases where willingness is low, EBP proponents need to recognize the process of implementing change will be a gradual one. Certain small areas of the organization will start to change, and when the benefits are realized and applauded, others take notice. The aim is to create a tipping point: 'that magical moment when an idea, trend, or social behaviour crosses a threshold, tips, and spreads like wildfire' (Gladwell, 2000: 4). In short, the groundwork for the cultural shift must be laid in a larger organization before resources are mobilized and/or generated.

One way of laying that groundwork is for police leaders and managers to instil a sense of purpose (Sinek, 2009). If you are working in policing and reading this, ask yourself, do you know what your purpose is? If not, the organization has failed in spreading the message of what it exists for. If you do, what was it that made that purpose stick in your mind? In his book, *Start with Why*, Simon Sinek (2009) explains that in many workforces most people know *what* they do, a larger proportion of people will know *what to do*, but few know *why* they do it. This question of 'why' is important in creating a police agency that is willing to think critically about its operations.

Assistant Chief Constable
Chris Noble
Humberside Police,
Hull, UK

A key challenge is how to embed a *culture* of challenge and innovation that is fundamental to the sustainable use of EBP. The danger is that large organizations 'project-ize' EBP and use it to cover off the requirement for benefits realization as opposed to adding to a body of policing knowledge and ensuring effective and ethical 'operational treatments'.

In Humberside, while key 'projects' such as body-worn video and domestic abuse triage teams are subject to evidence-based evaluations, the approach has been to develop a *program* of work and a comprehensive *partnership* with the University of Hull. This has seen all the faculties in the University meet with the commands in Humberside Police to identify opportunities for research, innovation and evaluation. The policing brain is fused with the academic, and the question is 'why wouldn't we [partner operational practice and academic rigour]?' as opposed to 'why should we?'

Early adopters

What is essential to the growth of EBP in any large policing organization is the presence of enthusiasts who are willing to drive an evidence-based agenda. We have seen this in larger US police organizations, including one within which a lieutenant was able to successfully help develop his organization's burgeoning EBP culture. To be clear: in this instance, the agency's chief was an early and solid supporter; however, it was the lieutenant who created an EBP working group, brought in outside trainers to educate the department on police science, facilitated discussions on EBP with community members, and established partnerships with the Vera Institute of Justice and the National Police Foundation.

Whereas early adopters in smaller agencies may have some degree of latitude in relation to being able to promote and/or implement elements of EBP, within larger agencies many advocates will find that a critical component for success is having some level of organizational support. This can be a significant challenge. To put the matter succinctly, high-level support for EBP is key because the politics of larger organizations can often be more complex and more challenging. Organizational leaders – like the chief described above – can show their support for their early adopters by creating an environment in which these enthusiasts flourish, allowing them the freedom to operate and the analytical support required to help them build robust trials of new ideas. While this level of support may sound like the stuff of fairy tales to some, we have seen examples of this in practice. For instance, with support from their executive, Thames Valley Police have developed their own policing journal written and edited by its own officers. They also have a thriving network of officers and staff who do policing research and hold regular conferences showcasing internal research to support their people. The use of internal conferences to showcase individual and group work is also commonplace in several other UK police agencies, such as Lancashire, Merseyside, Devon and Cornwall, Staffordshire, and Greater Manchester Police.

We have also seen examples where the early adopters were at opposite ends of the rank structure. The early adopters in the Portland Police Bureau were Chief Mike Reese and Sergeant Greg Stewart. Although this sounds like the perfect situation, sometimes having no support in the middle ranks can be a challenge. Having the chief as an EBP champion can be highly beneficial, but he or she often does not have the time to really garner support with the troops. The sergeant is in a different position; she or he may have time to garner the support, but possibly not the power or authority to move people in a new direction. Lack of support from a middle manager could lead to the movement not gaining any traction. The Portland Police Bureau was well on its way to becoming an EBP department, implementing their first RCT on community engagement in hotspots and training their executive command in EBP, when the chief retired. The new chief was not interested in research and the movement died. Recruiting early adopters throughout the ranks can help support the overall adoption of EBP over time.

Despite some of the political and other organizational challenges, there is one clear advantage to being an early adopter within a larger agency: the relative size of an organization may mean that other early adopters of EBP might number in the hundreds rather than being counted on one hand. The importance of having support from colleagues with similar views on police science cannot be understated. Each of us has stories about being waylaid at an event by an eager, if slightly frustrated, early adopter, who was keen to have someone with whom to share their interests. Having a group of early EBP supporters can ameliorate some of those feelings of isolation.

Having a cluster of like-minded supporters can also help to further the possibility of reaching a tipping point within the organization much sooner. That said, it would be challenging to provide support needed for every early adopter. This leads us to the question of how best to implement EBP within a larger agency. Should EBP be reserved for a chosen few specialists, such as crime analysts or sergeants? Or should it be a philosophy embraced by the whole agency? At a minimum, if a police agency wants to change its decision-making culture to one that relies on evidence, then everybody in that agency should have an awareness of EBP. This is not to say that everybody has to have a deep understanding, but everybody must understand what is meant by evidence in the context of EBP. And a good place to start is with the crime analysts.

Crime analysts

Larger agencies typically have crime analysts at the ready to inform the agency about anything crime-related. What distinguishes crime analysis in larger organizations is the number of available analysts: most larger services have entire departments focusing on crime analysis, as well as embedded analysts in patrol and intelligence divisions. That is a lot of additional research know-how. Unfortunately, despite this wealth of available knowledge, not all services utilize it wisely, and many analysts, including in larger organizations, remain relegated to purely operational roles producing basic crime stats and maps (Taylor et al, 2007; Piza and Feng, 2017), what some have termed 'wallpaper' (Innes et al, 2005). What analysts are often not provided with is the ability to engage in program evaluation or experimentation or other more critical analytical work (Piza and Feng, 2017; Green and Rossler, 2019), despite the fact that an increasing number support evidence-based approaches and the desire to improve the rigor of their work and produce more research-based products (Keay and Kirby, 2018).

When police services do get it right and create opportunities within which their analysts can engage in more demanding research, the results can be incredibly insightful. As an example, Elizabeth Macbeth, a Business Improvement Coordinator for the Police Service of Northern Ireland (PSNI), conducted research examining the ability of the PSNI's officers to predict crime concentrations, which were tested against statistical predictions. She and Barak Ariel found that the officers' waymarkers (the symbols the officers place on the maps to indicate crime hotspots) were nearly always misplaced, demonstrating that human intuition and experience is not always the soundest basis for preventative policing (Macbeth and Ariel, 2019). This is a significant discovery because so much of police work has been built on experience and intuition (Sherman, 2013), thus their work lends support for more evidence-based and data-driven approaches. It also highlights the importance of sound crime analysis.

Many crime analysts have the necessary skills to expand into new research methodologies if just given the opportunity. When the Portland police chief discovered EBP and wanted to implement a hotspots study, he reached out to the crime analysis sergeant, Greg Stewart. Sergeant Stewart had already previously engaged in a research partnership with a professor from Portland State University to create a risk assessment tool for domestic violence. His understanding of quantitative research and the established research partnership allowed for an easy transition into conducting a large, 90 hotspot RCT. Both Sergeant Stewart and his crime analyst, Christian Peterson, developed their analytical abilities through the implementation of quantitative studies and both became the National Institute of Justice's Law Enforcement Advancing Data and Science (LEADS) scholars.

Data and data tools

It would be fair to say that most larger police services collect, store, retain, and use a significant volume of data for operational purposes; with some ingenuity, much of it can also be used to address significant crime, administrative, and other issues police face. One fantastic example is the increasing use of body-worn video (BWV) for non-operational purposes. As an example, some services are now testing and/or using BWV as a training tool, providing supervisors with an opportunity to review interactions with the public and to offer feedback and correction (Nawaz and Tankebe, 2018; Pegram et al, 2018). Traditional methods of recording crimes and calls for service are now providing police services with the means of developing predictive analytics. In the UK, Durham Police was one of the first police agencies to look at predictive analytics, using an algorithm they called HART (Harm Assessment Risk Tool). HART is used in custody facilities in Durham to assess detainee risk and to help inform decision-making on potential release by the custody sergeant (Oswald et al, 2018). Kent Police has also experimented with predictive analysis, in their case, focusing on children at risk of witnessing domestic abuse. Detective Superintendent Andy Featherstone developed a model that tracked incidents over a two-and-a-half-year period, which he used to predict which children were most likely to view domestic abuse and thus would be in greatest need of services.

Crime analysts can also help develop tools to help their organization better understand their data and the software that is on the market. Crime analyst Tim Mashford from the Australian Police Service in Victoria developed a software program to test the predictive capability of a statistical tool (kernel density estimation, or KDE) using different time spans – 2, 4, 12 (3 months), 26 (6 months), 39 (9 months) and 52 weeks (1 year) – and varied the KDE parameter values (www.anzsebp.com/). He ran several iterations of the test using different combinations of time and parameter values. All in all, he ran 36 different tests and demonstrated that the longer the time period, 6 months and 1 year, and the larger the bandwidth, the better the predictive ability. Mashford was not able to compare his technique to PredPol or Risk Terrain Modeling software, thus it is unknown whether Mashford's software had better predictive ability than commercial software. He did demonstrate that police agencies could create a test to determine what method of KDE gives the best predictive capacity. Understanding how to get the most out of the resources available to an organization is an important component of policing. And testing a theory is an important component of EBP.

Another great example of the ability of police services to harvest not only their data but also the talents within their crime analysis sections is offered by Vancouver Police Department (VPD). VPD has a Crime Analytics Advisory & Development Unit, which is comprised of analysts tasked with developing new applications to assist patrol and intelligence operations. One of us, Laura, once observed a presentation of some of the Unit's work, which included hotspot maps 'pushed' down to patrol officers' mobile data terminals as reference guides when investigating, for example, area break and enters. Using its analysts and data wisely, VPD, too, is at the forefront of artificial intelligence and predictive analytics in Canada, experimenting with, among other things, early identification of offender patterns.

Creating more resources

One might reasonably question the need for larger agencies to create more resources when, comparatively speaking, they are typically better resourced than their smaller counterparts. In this instance we're talking about something that many larger agencies might not have, which is access to resources that will better equip them with the tools, skills, and knowledge to become more evidence-based. In the preceding sections we have shown how some of those resources do already exist but can be underutilized. In this section, we show how agencies can build on those existing strengths to promote evidence-based practices throughout the organization.

Basic evidence-based policing training

When it comes to the question of how best to establish training within a larger organization, one of the questions that must be grappled with is, who do you focus on first? Clearly, senior leaders will require a degree of knowledge in order to fully understand the capability of their evidence-based champions. Could senior managers give the support and direction to lower-ranking individuals engaged in evidence-based practices if they do not understand what they are doing?

In *Meltdown*, Clearfield and Tilcsik describe the failed Nasdaq (National Association of Securities Dealers Automated Quotations exchange) launch of Facebook's IPO (initial public offering) in 2012 (Clearfield and Tilcsik, 2018). When 11:05 rolled around and trading was supposed to begin, nothing happened. No one knew why. Nasdaq managers scrambled to figure out the problem with no understanding of how their technology worked. Programmers quickly realized the problem was the result of a validation check that senior Nasdaq managers had ordered removed. As a result, information wasn't being shared across programs and no trades were occurring. Clearfield and Tilcsik use this example to argue that a manager does not need to become a programmer, but they do need to understand their operational environment and how potential changes can impact that environment. In the case of introducing EBP into the policing operational environment, we suggest that training senior leaders in EBP may be the best place to start.

You might think about developing a masterclass in EBP for senior leaders. This will maximize the opportunity to bust any myths that exist around the use of evidence in policing and assist with cultural change at that senior officer level. The highest paid person's opinion, or the HiPPO principle, as it is known (Nisbett, 2015), is sure to stifle innovation and growth of EBP unless these senior leaders are exposed to the true ethos of EBP. Exposing senior leaders to EBP by way of a masterclass, workshop, or similar should help to make them feel comfortable with the benefits that research can bring to their decision-making and the decision-making of their colleagues. When fully aware of the benefits of what a network of EBP champions can bring to senior leaders, they can then act as a sponsor and ensure that the evidence-based champion can be used effectively.

The set-up of a research or EBP board is one method for helping to ensure proper EBP training is given to every individual in the organization. The research board could create a matrix to determine what skills, knowledge, and abilities the employees should retain, then, working backwards, determine what training the organization should engage in. This will allow organizations to determine what knowledge should be retained at what levels. Research boards should think about what tiers of expertise should be set up and what appropriate educational training should be given to those in accordance with their level of EBP responsibility. A strategic lead for EBP of executive level, a tactical lead, and a cohort of evidence-based mentors should be qualified to Master's degree level in a relevant research-based discipline. Data managers and analysts should also be educated in EBP techniques. Additional training and awareness sessions can be run in various ways – from briefings, bespoke training days, and evidence-based cafe workshops, for example, creating not only levels of expertise, but also levels of support for everybody who works in the agency.

To support those officers who have received EBP training and who are eager to carry on their progress, Greater Manchester Police (GMP) has created an evidence-based champions network of over 100 officers and staff. This network is responsible for sharing information with their peers and is spread across the whole agency. Each of the GMP EBP champions has been educated in evidence-based approaches to various levels (some hold a PhD). All have an appetite to change the agency into a thinking organization that puts informed decision-making at the forefront. The GMP EBP champions network grows annually as a week-long course is delivered to about 70 people every year, enabling new people to join the network. The EBP champions then have a quarterly get-together with a guest speaker, and present their recent work and a healthy discussion, often a debate, develops that is conducive to learning and sparks outbreaks of ideas. There is no recognition of rank at these meetings, and all EBP champions are treated equally, enabling a level playing field for all to air their opinions and have a voice.

The New Zealand Police has created an Evidence-Based Policing Centre (EBPC) assigning personnel, resources, and funding to support the incorporation of EBP into the entire police service. The Centre is a joint project between New Zealand Police, the University of Waikato, Vodafone New Zealand, and Environmental Science Research. The incorporation of evidence-based practices is included in the four-year business strategy that New Zealand Police has laid out for itself, called 'Our Business'. The Centre was created to develop the internal support needed for their four-year plan. It has a director, Chief Superintendent Bruce O'Brien, a civilian police manager, Simon Williams, several crime analysts, forensic specialists, researchers, and EBP leads. The EBP leads are of varying ranks; they are chosen for their progressive mindset and work throughout the entire country. The idea behind the structure of the Centre is to have support throughout the entire police agency, geographically and hierarchically.

Experiential learning

As we suggested in the previous section, creating a research board is a good way to help facilitate the understanding and use of EBP practices. The board should set the agency strategy for effective problem-solving and evidence-based research. Ideally, it should be comprised of influential people in the policing agency, those who can make decisions and/or who are well respected within the organization. It should also include those EBP champions who have a detailed understanding of EBP practices. This way, if there are board members who are influential but who have limited experience or understanding of EBP, they can be educated during the meetings and learn, along with the rest of the organization. It is important to make sure that the board has knowledge diversity and people of all ranks, thus no one person or group dominates the conversations, leading to groupthink. The goal of the research board meeting should be to oversee the governance of the EBP strategy in a larger policing organization.

The idea of establishing a research or EBP board was borne from an idea of one of the authors, Roger. Roger set up an

EBP board within the GMP to replace the existing research board that had existed solely to coordinate and/or commission external research. Recognizing the importance of encouraging research from within the organization, he approached GMP's Chief Constable, Ian Hopkins, and received support. To further this goal, Assistant Chief Constable Chris Sykes was appointed as the strategic lead for EBP. A similar model exists within Staffordshire Police, with Assistant Chief Constable Jenny Sims taking the role of strategic lead.

Assistant Chief Constable Chris Sykes, Greater Manchester Police, Manchester, UK

My role as the strategic lead for EBP in Greater Manchester Police (GMP) is to ensure that the EBP work we undertake, is in line with our force priorities. My role is to work with colleagues to remove any unnecessary organizational blockages that hinder the use of 'what works evidence' within the force, to improve the service we provide.

This involves persuading line managers to support the development of EBP by releasing our people for training and conferences to enhance their understanding of the field. EBP is fast becoming embedded in GMP, and I am proud to have been able to support the delivery of experiments that have yielded fantastic results and necessary learning.

It is so important that EBP has visible chief officer backing, as this approval empowers your people to push the boundaries and be more innovative in their thinking.

One of the central tasks of a research board is to evaluate research proposals to determine if they are a good fit for the agency's operational and administrative needs. These can be both internal proposals from police personnel as well as external proposals from academics and/or students. The GMP board provides three possible answers to research proposals:

- Approved (self-explanatory)
- Not approved (self-explanatory)
- Pending rework (with comments to help shape the research to agency need).

Providing feedback to the proposals allows applicants to massage their ideas and submit a better proposal next time. The research board should function like a good peer reviewer when rejecting proposals – they should explain what is valuable about the proposal, what needs more explanation, and/or why the proposal is not a good fit for the organization at this time.

When creating a research board, one function of the board is to strengthen links with local universities by allowing them to 'guest' at certain research board meetings and offer their insights. This would be mutually beneficial as the university representative gets to see first-hand how research is commissioned and approved, allowing them to understand what the agency is looking for, helping them shape the research question prior to submission, and the agency gets insights from a learned academic.

The GMP research board meets each month, creating both an overall structure to EBP efforts, as well as imbuing participants with a real sense of the importance of EBP as a core value of the organization. The research board can take the lead and direct what research is carried out and with which academic partner (if there is to be an academic partner), and create an EBP hub to monitor what research projects are occurring in the organization.

What is an EBP hub? In GMP, it is a centralized group comprised of one middle-ranking officer and two police staff members. These individuals centrally coordinate the research activity and are responsible for ensuring the board is attended, the internal website is up to date, support for the evidence-based champions network, latest evidence-based findings email distribution, coordination of conference attendance, assistance with reviewing of internal funding bids to ensure plans have an evidence base or seek to develop one, and much more. In short, their goal is to support both the research board and ensure GMP's EBP mission is promoted throughout the organization. We will have more to say about EBP hubs shortly.

Building a library

Building a library in larger police organizations is difficult due to the sheer size of the organization and the obvious limitations to people being able to access centrally housed resources. One solution is to reward and recognize people with books that will spark interest in EBP, similar to the 'Leaders are Readers' programme in GMP. This program rewards police officers and staff who have contributed to EBP with books that support the growth of EBP and foster a curious mindset. Another option would be to have multiple libraries housed at a district level. This could be coordinated by the evidence-based champions who would be responsible for the upkeep of these district-based libraries and a central point of contact to receive books from the EBP hub. New book titles could be discussed at the EBP board, and agreements made by that board as to what should be purchased and added to the libraries paid for by central funds.

Equally, the EBP hub should be sharing book titles and research findings of interest on the internal website and via email to the EBP champions network for wider dissemination. To ensure these books are read and discussed, a book review could be requested from any individual in the organization and posted on the internal website to raise awareness of the EBP libraries. Guest lectures within police agencies are also a great way of authors/academics talking about their research findings, and often lead to energizing Q&A sessions.

Incorporating a little, some, or a lot of EBP

We realize that some of the obstacles with larger agencies are due to size. It can take longer to get a larger ship on course, and having widespread adoption of EBP throughout an organization with several thousand employees will necessarily take some time. We have each seen examples where larger agencies have been trying to incorporate EBP into their practice for a couple of years, and it is not at all unusual to continue to see senior leaders within such organizations advocating for more 'boots on the ground' as an 'evidence-based' remedy to a crime spike. Thus, not only will EBP adoption not happen overnight; it may not happen over a decade. That said, there are ways in which people, groups, and organizations can incorporate a little, some, or a lot of EBP into their practices.

Systematic literature reviews

Ensuring people in large policing agencies have access to academic literature with which to conduct systematic literature reviews can be problematic, with many articles being hidden behind paid firewalls. As noted in previous chapters, it is possible to access subscription-only journals and articles through local libraries. In the UK, the College of Policing has a facility where all members receive online access similar to that of a university student. The New Zealand EBPC commissions systematic reviews on topics of interest to the organization. It contracts with various universities to complete them and then post them in its EBP portal. Every employee of New Zealand Police has access to the EBP portal, making the dissemination of the systematic reviews relatively easy.

Of course, having access alone does not assist individuals with conducting a literature review. Fortunately, there are resources available. Can-SEBP has a brief video on conducting systematic reviews, as well as a more detailed 'hands-on' video for using Zotero, free software that allows users to archive articles for a possible literature review. Further, many larger organizations have individuals within them who have engaged in academic studies and who can provide support. As an example, the EBP hub in GMP has assisted the evidence-based champions in examining the current literature so that no random research projects are started without any thought to what is already known. The evidence-based champions meet centrally every quarter to discuss what worked, what didn't, and what's promising. When a research project comes to an end, the EBP champion is expected to start another, and this sets in motion another systematic review of the existing literature that is pertinent to the particular area of the business or problem they are seeking to improve. The EBP hub, tactical lead, crime analyst, and lead or subject matter expert will review the existing evidence and then seek to design an intervention that helps build on that evidence base, or endeavour to plug the gap in the evidence.

Program evaluation

One way to make sense of program evaluation is to create an EBP hub. This will be the central repository of completed research, research that is underway, and/or approved research plans that have yet to start. The EBP hub also acts as a conduit between parties that have similar research interests. While duplicate tests are not a bad thing – replication being a key to creating an evidence base – for certain subject areas, a service may not wish to invest in two or more pieces of research on the same topic. The EBP hub will mitigate any of this unwanted duplication, while providing timely updates of progress to the 'EBP board'; this will allow that board to make an informed decision on whether it wants to commission another piece of research that may support the ongoing research area.

The EBP hub should have an internal webspace where it can publish information to the organization about what is currently happening, and give its people a point of reference to find information. The internal website could take many forms, but the following list of information should be readily available:

- A message from the strategic lead and the tactical lead.
- A synopsis of what EBP is.
- Contact details of the EBP hub staff (email addresses and telephone numbers).
- A list of the EBP board members.
- A list of the EBP champions.
- Upcoming key events.

- Examples of EBP in action.
- Examples of that agency's learning from EBP.
- Information on how to get involved.
- Frequently asked questions.
- Links to other sites that support EBP.

The EBP hub should contain information about program evaluation, explaining the differences between research methods. A description of the Maryland Scientific Methods Scale (SMS) should be presented on the site, with a link to the original paper (see https://whatworksgrowth.org/ for a link to a more detailed example). Similar to the Ratcliffe hierarchy discussed in Chapter 3, the Maryland SMS, created by Farrington and colleagues (2002), sets out five levels of quantitative scientific research in terms of increasing rigorousness of the methods used. Level 1 is a study that simply tries to calculate the effects of a program intervention by measuring changes after the implementation. This type of research can be contrasted to Level 2 (what we call a 'pre- or post-test' design), which compares possible effects after the implementation of a program to conditions before the implementation. Level 3 is a study design that adds in control factors and conditions to reduce the possibility that other, extraneous, factors might be causing any changes observed, whereas Level 4 builds on the previous study design by adding in additional testing and control sites. Level 5 is the standard RCT, which, of course, adds an element of randomization to the process to try to limit the possibility of bias in the study or its results.

Experiments

Experiments are a fantastic tool to determine effectiveness and efficiency of practices within a larger organization, as well as a means of determining whether an intervention creates harm to the community (McCord, 2003). And, given the greater resources that a larger organization typically commands, very few lack the internal resources or the ability to access external partnerships that would justify *not* conducting tests of new policies and programs.

In recent years police-led field experiments have gathered momentum at a fast pace globally, with experiments informing policing on important findings often building on research previously conducted by academics, such as that of Simon Williams, now a serving officer in New Zealand, who researched the optimum length and frequency of hotspot patrols in Birmingham in the UK (Williams and Coupe, 2017). The purpose of the experiment was to determine whether shorter, more frequent patrol visits to the same crime hotspots are more effective in reducing crime and anti-social behaviour (ASB) compared to longer, less frequent visits, keeping total patrol time constant. The independent variable, time spent by an officer within seven geo-fenced hotspots, was calculated based on GPS measures from their body-worn radio. The dependent variable was calculated based on the total number of daily crime and ASB reports within the hotspots. The target 45 minutes of daily patrolling was broken down into two patrol duration conditions: long visits (three visits of 15 minutes each) and short visits (nine visits of 5 minutes each) assigned randomly to each hotspot daily. Results suggested that controlling for total daily patrol time, longer visits (10–15 minutes) led to 20 percent less crime compared to shorter visits.

Similarly, Commander Alex Murray of the Metropolitan Police ran an experiment on the optimum number of properties to visit to reduce repeat/near repeat burglary in Birmingham (Johnson et al, 2017). The experiment evaluated a police-led target-hardening crime prevention strategy related to space–time patterns of burglary, and involved 46 West Midlands neighbourhoods in the UK that were randomly assigned treatment and control conditions. The treatment areas were provided with inexpensive target-hardening resources and dedicated police advice, and the effectiveness of the measures was evaluated through a resident survey. Results revealed that within the treatment group, residents were relatively more satisfied with the police as they had likely been contacted in relation to the burglaries and were less fearful, despite having greater awareness of the crime. Results also showed a modest yet positive effect of interventions on crime and revictimization rates in low crime areas compared to those with higher crime rates.

In another experiment, Assistant Chief Constable Scott Chilton (former chair of the SEBP in the UK) of Hampshire Police, together with others from Hampshire Police, ran an experiment looking at ways of reducing intimate partner violence (Strang et al, 2017). The purpose was to determine whether randomly assigning males who have been involved in first-time low-risk intimate partner violence to two day-long Cautioning and Relationship Abuse (CARA) workshops would reduce the total severity of crime compared to the control group. The primary outcome measure for each of the 293 randomly assigned offenders based on repeat arrests or complaints was coded using the Cambridge Crime Harm Index (CHI). The total number of recommended days of imprisonment for each offence was summed across all new domestic and non-domestic offences along with prevalence and frequency of repeat contact. Results found CARA workshops to be effective in reducing future incidents of domestic abuse among offenders who admit their crime.

Merseyside Police conducted Operation Reddlemen using this experiment to discover they could maintain service levels with fewer resources when policing the night-time economy in Liverpool (Gibson et al, 2017). For the experiment, police presence was measured every 5 minutes via GPS for five pairs of geo-fenced hotspots, along with crime incident data for two nights over six consecutive weekends. These data were matched with the same 12 nights one year earlier and two nights two weeks before the experiment. The Maryland SMS Level 4 test was employed as the research design in which the five experimental hotspots received 12–15 minutes of patrol every hour compared to higher levels of patrol in the control group. Results revealed that the total incidents reported to the police in the five experimental group hotspots were reduced compared to the control group, which led to 40 percent cost savings for the experimental group.

GMP conducted an innovative experiment to reduce the number of incidences of Missing from Home (MfH) from care homes in order to protect the child residents from harm (Pegram, 2018). A care home with a recurring MfH problem was identified, and the GMP commissioned an analyst to review the number of calls for service and the number of MfH reports from the care home over three years. The experiment was based on purchasing a Netflix subscription for the care home and to supply a takeaway one night of the week. For four months the staff filled out a tracking form with information on who ate what, who stayed in, who engaged, who didn't engage, and so on. The project cost to the GMP was £50 per week and the results showed a 50 percent reduction in MfH compared to 2017, which equates to £239,085 in savings (£2,415 per MfH) for GMP. There was a significant reduction in calls for service overall by 49 percent in that four-month period.

In the USA, the Metropolitan Police Department in Washington, DC carried out a large-scale field experiment with 2,224 officers to study the effect of body-worn cameras on civilian–police interactions (Yokum et al, 2019). Officers were randomly assigned to receive cameras and their behaviour was tracked for seven months using administrative data. Results indicated that cameras did not affect police behaviour significantly, especially on outcomes such as complaints and use of force, concluding that cameras had a smaller impact than expected.

In another place-based, randomized experiment conducted in the USA, the Philadelphia Police Department explored the impact of different patrol strategies on violent and property crime in predicted crime areas using a predictive policing software program (Ratcliffe et al, 2020). Twenty Philadelphia city districts were randomized to receive three interventions that included awareness districts with officers aware of predicted areas; districts with marked cars assigned to treatment areas; and districts with unmarked cars. Routine response was assigned to the control condition. Results showed that only the marked car intervention led to a 31 percent reduction in expected property crime, with a 40 percent reduction in expected crime count in the subsequent eight-hour shift.

In Australia, the Queensland Police Service (QPS) designed a special purpose-built van, the Mobile Police Community Office (MPCO). The van was to function as a mobile police station in Brisbane for crime reduction and enhancement of public engagement based on principles of procedural justice

(Bennett et al, 2017). To test the effectiveness of the MPCO, an experiment was conducted by matching 24 hotspots based on crime and location characteristics. The hotspots were randomly assigned within pairs to either the existing police response or the existing response in addition to the MPCO for two days. A public survey was administered to assess the perception of police legitimacy. The results of pre-/post-deployment suggested a modest yet insignificant decrease in crime, and no evidence of a reduction in police legitimacy. However, further testing and replication of the study is required over a longer period to determine the value of such efforts. These and similar other examples essentially examine the effective use of police resourcing, how long to stay at a hotspot, how many houses to visit, which offenders to target, and so on. This focus on targeting with precision to more effectively deploy limited resources is critical for many services given years of budget and resource cuts.

It is evident that much of policing demand is not solely the responsibility of policing but also creeps into the space of other services. True collaborative partnerships require coordination and a performance framework that all parties agree to (Dupont, 2004). This 'networked' approach can work, which has been evidenced by research into incidents of ASB in Leeds where a collaborative approach was taken, gathering housing providers, local authorities, and youth justice workers to identify young people's needs. This collaborative effort helped the participants understand the problem and made them better at delivering and evaluating a preventative intervention. This study found that a well-organized effective partnership can reduce crime and improve community safety (Crawford, 2009).

In addition to partnerships, policing itself has a number of subject matter experts in many different disciplines. Tapping into these experts to assist with experimentation is critical. Many of these experts have in-depth knowledge about a variety of topics such as domestic abuse, mental health, hate crime, firearms, and public order policing. Equally, a number of 'pracademics' in a large policing agency can act as mentors to the evidence-based champions. These 'pracademics' can help with the framing of research questions and assist the EBP champions in defining their problem and setting out methods of how they can test interventions and measure what happens. This method of peer-to-peer mentoring of people within the agency shows that research can involve everybody, helping to build trust and better relations between those who are already involved and those who are showing interest.

Pracademics can most often help develop an organization's internal capabilities in EBP because they already come imbued with 'street cred'. One of the pracademics we have discussed throughout this chapter, Simon Williams, initially began his career at West Midlands Police in Birmingham, UK. While he was a student at the University of Cambridge, he conducted an RCT on hotspots policing comparing the outcomes between visiting the hotspots for more time and less visits versus more visits and for less time (Williams and Coupe, 2017). He developed his ability to conduct field experiments to such an extent he was recruited to the Western Australia Police as a senior sergeant to lead their EBP division, and eventually to New Zealand Police to develop their expertise in their new Evidence-Based Policing Centre. Having an officer who can develop a research methodology skill set is invaluable for an organization that wants to learn what works, what doesn't, and what we should be improving on.

Summing up

This chapter has explored the differing elements of how a larger police organization could seek to successfully adopt an evidence-based approach to the way it operates. We have drawn from evidence of other agencies that have excelled in embedding EBP in their decision-making and in creating a culture of curiosity among their people. We note, however, that although larger police services often have the financial and human resources to develop and test their own innovations, they are not necessarily open to change. We argue the importance of laying a solid foundation to creating cultural change by identifying strategies for motivating internal stakeholders while dealing with institutional bureaucracy. High-level support for EBP can be achieved through training of top management, as well as using crime analysts to engage in more demanding research. We also recommend developing a masterclass in EBP for senior leaders and establishing an EBP board to determine the skills, knowledge, and training the organization should engage in. Rewarding evidence-based practices and ensuring people in large policing agencies have access to academic literature through a central repository, along with experimentation, can also prove instrumental in embedding EBP practices.

While there is no blueprint to guaranteed success, ensuring that these principles are followed will help to replicate some of the successes that have been realized by those larger agencies that are well on their way to becoming 'totally evidenced' organizations.

8

Generating sustainability

As we've observed with numerous policing initiatives over the years, programs can quickly become derailed as a result of a lack of forethought to the issue of long-term sustainability (Willis et al, 2007; Bradley and Nixon, 2009; Kalyal et al, 2018). Of all the topics we cover in this book, this is likely the one that is easiest to describe in theory but that will generate the most difficulty in practice. The reason for this is simple: the adoption of evidence-based policing (EBP) requires not only a degree of investment in individuals as change agents, but also, for some agencies, what might appear to be a radical rethinking of how police services engage in decision-making. While we recognize that the exigencies of policing can sometimes be best met by the traditional command and control structure, an evidence-based organization is one that embodies a learning culture – that is, an institutional culture that places emphasis on seeing operational and administrative decisions as opportunities for implementing innovation and learning lessons from both success and failure. It is also one that requires a more decentralized approach to viewing expertise and soliciting input and feedback into decision-making. In this chapter, we draw on the relevant management and other literatures, as well as on our own and others' experiences, to make some specific and some broader recommendations for how to generate a sustainable EBP approach within small organizations.

Practical solutions

Investing in internal resources

A study was recently published showing that police officers experience increased job satisfaction when engaged in problem-solving activities within their communities (Sytsma and Piza, 2018). This should hardly be surprising. When organizations hire intelligent, thoughtful, analytical people with diverse knowledge and skills, those same people want to do work that is both intellectually and emotionally satisfying. Or, as one of us recently posted, 'let smart people do smart work.'

The reality, however, can be very different. Another study, this one on crime analysts, revealed that very few of those surveyed were involved in program evaluation or other forms of experimentation (Piza and Feng, 2017). As the authors suggest – and we agree – this is a tremendous waste of internal resources (Piza and Feng, 2017), and can lead to some analysts feeling their work is little more than 'wallpaper' (Innes et al, 2005: 52). In many countries, crime analysts come to their positions with graduate-level training in research. We know of police services with individuals with not one Master's degree but two and/or a doctorate. That is a lot of research talent being wasted. This is no less the case for police officers. We routinely encounter police officers with phenomenal analytical skills, not all of whom have graduate training, but who do understand logic models, how to operationalize research methodology, and who can provide wisdom and insight into how best to commission, create, and/or use research. This is more talent frequently wasted.

So what is our solution? Police services can begin by identifying those people within their organizations who can serve not only as internal resources, but also as role models to others who might potentially be interested in EBP. Once you have taken this step, help to facilitate their growth by not only providing opportunities to engage in research (either internally or with external partners), but also work to facilitate their access to relevant training and education in new areas. Even the most experienced PhD-laden crime analyst could and would benefit from flexing their intellectual muscles by learning new analytical software, new research techniques, or taking on new subjects.

If that person who needs some intellectual stretching is you, then the advice is the same: invest in yourself or convince others to do that for or with you. And again, don't be put off if you don't have a college degree – many EBP champions had no formal college or university education before they began implementing research in their organizations. Over the course of a long policing career, officers are exposed to all types of training courses, which can prepare them for more advanced training. There are several modes of training available, from online to in-person courses, to intensive courses where students stay on campus for a longer duration such as multiple weeks or even months. Typically, training courses are structured for people at different levels of understanding – it is just a matter of finding a course that fits the student's ability and availability. For example, a simple Google search can generate multiple leads for courses on the internet or near your location. The University of Waterloo in Canada offers a two-day course that teaches students how to 'automate literature reviews for knowledge discovery and synthesis'. This course assists students in learning how to efficiently do a literature review to get up to speed on a vast field of knowledge. This type of course would be beneficial to any person interested in delving into a new research topic, as it would teach them how to immerse themselves in the knowledge of the field without wasting time or becoming overwhelmed by the magnitude of information. Two days is not a significant expenditure of police resources or so intensive that you should feel discouraged from attending. Nor should the fact that it's a university course be a deterrent for anyone. Realizing that smaller police services could benefit from the University of Waterloo's course, Laura reached out to the instructor and asked one simple question: 'Would you accept police employees in these courses?' The answer: 'Yes'.

Training courses for police officers or crime analysts do not necessarily have to be only one or two days. If possible, longer-term training programs can increase an employee's ability when the courses are intensive. One of the most well-known programs for training social scientists can also be found on the internet, the Inter-University Consortium for Political and Social Research (ICPSR). The Summer Program in Quantitative Methods of Research is held at the University of Michigan in the USA, and offers a wide variety of classes for researchers, no matter the level of expertise. Scholarships are available to students who cannot afford the courses and a discount to students whose agencies are part of the ICPSR network. They offer two formats for their program: short workshops and four-week sessions. The short workshops are offered in the USA, Canada, and Europe. The courses range from introductory courses such as Mathematics for Social Scientists to Hierarchical Linear Modeling for advanced students who want to take their training to the next level.

In-house researchers

A prerequisite for advancing EBP is for police management to have a genuine understanding of research, the conditions under which evidence is produced, and how such evidence may contribute to practice. For police research to flourish, we must strive to foster contexts where the police and academia can establish long-standing collaborative arrangements, both of which benefit according to their different needs and perspectives (Madensen and Sousa, 2015; Knutsson and Tompson, 2017). This can be done by incorporating an in-house researcher into the organization. We have seen this occur in a couple of different ways. One way is to hire a criminologist to work in a police department, paying their salary, providing an office, computer, analytical software, and so on (Taniguchi and Bueermann, 2012). Another way is buying out a university professor's or researcher's time from the university to work in conjunction with the police department (Braga, 2013). The intent of both approaches is to move an agency towards evidence-based practices by developing institutional knowledge about police research and research methods, for the criminologist to contribute to policy development, evaluate practice, and contribute to organizational understanding of EBP. These efforts will help shift the organizational culture away from a traditional approach to a scientific one.

The intention with applied police research is to provide the police with policy-relevant research evidence. It means, to put it somewhat pointedly, research carried out for and with the police (Cockbain and Knutsson, 2015). 'With the police' means letting police practitioners choose the areas of research they would like to pursue. Successful situations involving the embedding of criminologists usually occur when the police agency is driving the topics of research (Frisch, 2016). Giving police ownership over the research creates buy-in, especially if the research topic addresses a long-standing issue the organization is dealing with, such as gun crime (Braga, 2013).

Another way in which to increase successful collaboration is through ensuring the researcher has a place within the police department, allowing them into command staff meetings, having them go on ride-a-longs and sit-a-longs. Each of these measures goes a long way towards building a sustainable EBP model. Constant contact and conversation creates an opportunity for the researcher to build a long-standing relationship with the police, to have more direct access to the organization and its data, and thus to be in an advantageous position to support the police with research evidence (Frisch, 2016).

External research relationships

Not every agency has the resources to fund a full-time research position. In Chapter 5 we discussed how smaller agencies can leverage external expertise by partnering with researchers who may or may not be local. As most mid-sized agencies will be located in cities or towns with local colleges or universities, our focus here is slightly different. What we suggest is developing long-term relationships with one or more local researchers. Many researchers have a specific area they research, such as deterrence, life course development, procedural justice, or implicit bias. Even though an organization may have a relationship with one researcher, they may want to evaluate a topic that is not the researcher's area of expertise, which can lead to developing relationships with multiple researchers rather than just one. Technology allows us to have research relationships with people who live anywhere in the world. One of the authors, Renée, formed a partnership with researchers in another US state to run her Sacramento Hot Spots study. The relationship was forged at the American Society of Criminology conference but continued with ongoing phone conversations afterwards, which led to partnering on the study. Partnerships can be structured in any way that the researcher and practitioners find beneficial.

To illustrate one way in which this relationship can be structured: one of us, Laura, is the 'Research Fellow' for a mid-sized municipal police service that also happens to be her own local police agency. The creation of the Research Fellow position came as a result of discussions on how best to help police agencies generate research in ways that could be beneficial for both police practitioners and researchers. The Research Fellow position was established as a voluntary, pro bono role that includes the following responsibilities:

• Conducting independent research at the police service (subject to necessary approvals).
• Conducting special internal research projects (as necessary).
• Providing consultative services to service personnel on research and educational issues.
• Providing expertise on the development of research projects and educational programs for the service.
• Evaluating, assisting, facilitating, and otherwise working with or in support of other researchers and the service to ensure quality research production at the service.

The initial tenure for this position was set at one year, with the possibility of annual renewals. Having an annual renew or some other time frame is a good idea, as both the researcher and the police service can terminate any relationships that don't appear to be working well. In Laura's case, she is going on to her fourth year with this agency, and they have run about half a dozen projects during this time, with more in the pipeline.

Other agencies prefer to work with multiple researchers as a means of acquiring diverse expertise. In such cases, it is necessary to have someone within the agency who is well-versed in research and who can serve as a central point of contact for researchers, as well as being responsible for administering research agreements and providing general oversight of research conduct within the organization. They will also need to serve as a gatekeeper, controlling access to policing resources. We have seen this in police agencies, where they have specific problems or interventions they want evaluated. Examining the research field, they choose to reach out to multiple researchers rather than having one point of contact. One agency has employed researchers from a university two hours away, a university researcher in another state, and a local research group to examine separate issues in the agency. The topics range from police–citizen interactions, implicit bias training, and training issues in general. The organization obtained multiple researchers due to expertise in the different areas, rather than staying with one researcher to evaluate multiple topics.

Although it is suggested that this gatekeeper should have knowledge of police research, it is often assigned to the person who is managing a planning and research division, or someone who is running the crime analysis unit. The dream is to have someone with the background to understand police research, but the reality is that whatever manager is attached to the unit will be the person involved. If possible, assisting this person in their personal education of police research would be beneficial to the department, otherwise the department is left with the gatekeeper using their personal beliefs about what constitutes police research. And the police often obtain their 'research' from professional publications such as *Police Chief Magazine*, the *FBI Law Enforcement Bulletin*, and other publications from the International Association of Chiefs of Police (Alpert et al, 2013). This shows that the police do not generally find their research in empirical journals, and rely on sources for research information that are not peer-reviewed. Having a staff member who is unaware of the difference between good research and poor research as your gatekeeper can be problematic. We would suggest that if your gatekeeper is going to work with multiple researchers, then that person should be well-educated on research methodology.

Working groups

Internal working group can be a great method for generating new ideas, inculcating an evidence-based approach to decision-making, identifying current and potential pracademics, and building cohesion among EBP practitioners. That said, they also require an investment in time and energy, especially in the early development stages, to build the trust necessary for individuals to be willing to share ideas and therefore risk criticism. This model may work well with police agencies, as this is a traditional format for implementing new programs or projects. Titling an EBP effort as a working group may seem less intimidating than trying to create an EBP unit or embed a researcher. A working group feels less formal, and people may be more willing to participate.

It is something of a criminal justice axiom that police officers never raise their hands to volunteer answers or ideas in groups. Each of us has seen this repeatedly in training scenarios where questions to generate audience participation draw blank looks, averted eyes, and/or hands decidedly nowhere near an upright position. In fact, our colleague, Natalie Hiltz, has a useful analogy for explaining this phenomenon: she likens it to those wildlife specials where, invariably, some cute animal gets eaten. Here's Natalie's explanation:

Staff-Sergeant
Natalie Hiltz,
Peel Regional Police
Service, Ontario, Canada

It's a case of 'monkeys versus alligators'. A typical episode on a *National Geographic*-type show: during drought season all the animals find themselves by a river bed trying to survive. The monkeys are thirsty. As soon as one gets brave enough to break off from the group to get some water, an alligator ALWAYS gets them. While they're getting ripped to shreds, dying a painful death, none of the other monkeys ever comes to help. They huddle closer together and watch the carnage. It's an important lesson: never stray from the group. Don't be vulnerable, because when you get bit, nobody is coming to help you. Whatever you choose to do in life, always stay with the group.

This phenomenon, by the way, is hardly unique to policing. A significant body of evidence exists to show that humans tend towards conformity and can fear being a dissenting voice or risking real or perceived social status through speaking up (Kaplan, 2017; Nemeth, 2018). We've certainly seen this repeatedly in undergraduate classrooms, graduate seminar rooms, public venues, and so on. It's driven by the fear of saying something that might be wrong (venturing too far out) and that might make you look foolish to peers or bosses (the snap of alligator jaws). That said, our own experience, and some new research (Wieslander, 2018), suggests such fears are particularly acute within the institution of policing. This fear has to be overcome, however, if a working group is going to be free enough with each other to share ideas, offer, and receive constructive criticism – that is, to engage in the basics tasks necessary to generating research. So how to overcome this?

One solution is to identify influencers or leaders within the group who will drive the discussion, generate ideas, and work to ensure individuals have roles to play. One of us found out how important influencer-leaders are to creating group cohesion the hard way. Laura works with an agency that had just set up an internal working group. Seeing herself as a facilitator of *their* group, she asked to establish a WhatsApp group to help share ideas. When their original study was delayed due to external factors, she turned to WhatsApp to ask the group, 'who has any ideas for another study?' This query generated radio silence. For days. Rather than giving up (admittedly her first impulse), she asked Natalie for some advice. The issue was, she needed to shift her own cultural perspective. As an academic, she is used to being a facilitator, but this group needed a leader. As new members of an EBP initiative, they needed an initial structure to work within, as well as active mentoring. Once that explanation gelled, Laura took the lead, getting back onto the group chat to suggest specific research topics and to solicit their thoughts. Within 30 seconds of that text, the first answer came in. Then a second. What did we learn? It's not realistic to expect people to spontaneously adopt and execute an approach. There's a learning curve and working groups – individual members, and the group as a whole – need active mentoring to get them to the point of being comfortable contributing to group discussions.

Some other good ideas:

- Leave your rank at the door. This idea comes from Roger, who has observed that to create an ethos of sharing, people have to feel free to speak up and, when necessary, critique others' ideas. We note it can be very difficult to do this in any hierarchical organization, but the command and control structure of policing adds an additional limiting factor on that willingness.
- Make use of mobile technology. WhatsApp and other communication-sharing platforms on hand-held devices allow EBP groups to stay connected, no matter what shifts individuals are working.
- Use conference software. Skype, FaceTime and other software allow for more flexibility in scheduling face-to-face discussion (when needed) than in-person meetings.
- Don't ask questions to the whole group as it leaves an individual to answer in front of the group and share their knowledge or lack thereof. Adult learners don't like to reveal their level of knowledge in front of others. Ask a question and have the group turn to the person next to them to discuss it. Then ask what the group thinks. This creates anonymity, and when someone speaks up, no one knows if it was their idea or their partner's.

Evidence-based policing units

In Sherman's paper, 'A tipping point for "totally evidenced policing"', he advocates for the adoption of EBP units staffed with 'evidence cops' who will support the use of EBP practices

(Sherman, 2015). To our knowledge, no police service has – to date – created an entire unit dedicated to this work, although several police organizations in Australia, Canada, New Zealand, and the UK do have a dedicated staff member who functions as an 'evidence cop', internal EBP working groups, and/or future plans to build such units.

Why an entire unit? A dedicated group would, in theory, serve an entire organization by guiding the implementation of EBP. The unit could employ a range of methods in its approach, as suggested by Sherman. It could compile the police research into different topic areas, possibly creating a library or online resource for the organization to access up-to-date research on policing. It could arrange masterclasses in its organization, either by teaching the material itself, or bringing in outside academics to teach the courses. Sherman suggests other steps such as: establishing a peer review process, sending a 'power few' to a Master's degree-level program, creating a central registry of EBP projects, and offering annual prizes for authors of the best EBP project (Sherman, 2015). The unit's responsibility would be to identify gaps in knowledge and build resources or classes to help bridge those knowledge gaps. It would be endowed with 'the responsibility of imposing an "evidence based lens" on decisions, policies, and programs, or some other techniques not yet identified' (Cordner, 2018). Officers could also work closely with the EBP unit in proposing and designing research projects, enabling them to develop a clear understanding and appreciation of the research process and acceptance of EBP practices. These suggestions are good guidelines for an agency that wants to identify areas of improvement, build internal knowledge of EBP, and implement rigorous evaluations of their practices.

Holistic solutions

Shifting to EBP will require a cultural change in most policing agencies. The pace at which an organization's culture evolves depends on its capacity for knowledge acquisition, that is, its ability to adopt and incorporate knowledge (Belkhodja et al, 2007). It is due to this difference that police agencies vary in their ability to adopt change. Changes such as EBP implementation tend to be time-consuming as they require a shift in cultural norms that are not easily modified. Greater acceptance of EBP may be possible if these initiatives are internally driven and do not conflict with organizational culture and identity. To achieve this goal, there is a need to create a cultural shift in favour of EBP through education and communication. Police culture prevents officers from being more proactive and providing hasty responses to oversight bodies for service improvements. EBP requires a major effort and a shift in thinking, especially for those who believe that they are incredibly successful in the way they manage their daily affairs. Therefore, some officers believe that EBP practices are likely to gather momentum with the retirement of older officers, making way for more educated ones who would be receptive to EBP. Max Planck, the originator of modern quantum theories, once said, 'A new scientific truth does not triumph by convincing its opponents and making them see the light, but rather because its opponents eventually die, and a new generation grows up that is familiar with it' (Planck, 1949: 33–4). For those of us who would prefer to see change occur at a quicker pace, we need to generate ideas about how to gain a cultural shift within our current generation of criminal justice professionals.

*Commander
Rachel Tolber,
Redlands Police
Department,
California, USA*

The question of how to sustain evidence-based practice is frequently asked in research and practitioner circles. Chief Bueermann (Retired), a well-known EBP advocate, ensured sustainability of EBP in the Redlands Police Department using both internal and external anchors. We educated both our employees and the community about various projects and practices that we were researching and implementing. We have continued to spend a good deal of time communicating and collaborating with our community. Our crime data is available to the community via crimemapping.org and we regularly release our crime statistics. We reward evidence-based practices, critical thinking, and innovation through technology throughout our department. These rewards exist as both the ability to participate in projects as well as in more formal ways such as promotion. Both involvement in and understanding of these concepts are part of our continual dialogue, practice, and reward structures in the hope of building a sustainable culture.

Creating a culture of learning

Many organizations today, both in the public and private sectors, are set up as 'learning organizations', that is, as organizations dedicated to innovation through a continual focus on learning. Perhaps the best description of this term is that offered by Peter Senge (1990: 3):

> ... organizations where people continually expand their capacity to create the results they truly desire, where new and expansive patterns of thinking are nurtured, where collective aspiration is set free, and where people are continually learning to see the whole together.

Such organizations not only foster spaces within which people can openly share ideas and collaborate, exposing themselves to new modes of thinking and technologies, but also treat all experiences as potential learning opportunities. One of the most famous examples of creating such a culture, and deliberately designing spaces to support that culture, and thus innovation through collaboration, is the site known as 1 Infinite Loop. When Apple moved into 1 Infinite Loop, its then new headquarters in Cupertino, California, the notoriously detail-oriented Steve Jobs had insisted on a design plan that would force workers in different parts of the business, who might otherwise never see each other, to come together, sometimes in unique ways (Isaacson, 2011). While we do not recommend designing centralized washrooms in one common area to force people from different floors to interact, we do think any efforts at dispelling silos across groups is helpful to producing an environment in which people can learn from each other and co-produce solutions and ways to test their ideas (see also Tett, 2016).

Another way in which organizations can support a learning environment is through rethinking what constitutes success and failure. In his pivotal book, *Black Box Thinking*, Matthew Syed (2015) uses the airline industry's approach to accident investigation as an excellent example of how to improve something (in this case, airline safety) through learning from system, individual, and other types of failure. It will come as no surprise to anyone in policing to be told that police organizations are not typically known as sites for calm, detached, methodical discussions on program, policy, or system failures. However, like Syed, we argue that they should be. In fact, we also argue that failure is often much more instructive than success:

> At the level of the brain, the individual, the organisation and the system, failure is a means – sometimes the only means – of learning, progressive and becoming more creative. This is a hallmark of science, where errors point to how theories can be reformed; of sport, where practice could be defined as the willingness to clock up well-calibrated mistakes; of aviation, where every accident is harnessed as a means of driving system safety. (Syed, 2015: 147)

We have discussed multiple ways to educate a police agency, both in this chapter and previous chapters. One of the strongest ways to educate a workforce is to have key influencers modelling the desired behaviour. With EBP, that can occur through having individuals creating or co-producing research (internally or with external academic support). In the same vein, learning can occur through officers and crime analysts sharing their research projects with others in the organization. Sharing case studies and success stories of EBP implementation within the department would also allow officers, crime analysts, planners, and others, to broaden their thought processes or to open them up a little more to something they've typically been reluctant to engage in (Sherman, 2015). Watching a co-worker present on a project they participated in demonstrates an organizational commitment to research. It allows officers to see someone like themselves expand their skills, knowledge, and ability. It sends the message to the organization that this is the behaviour the organization wants. This helps employees integrate EBP with their own experiences, thereby allowing for greater acceptance of change and improved decision-making.

Another important factor influencing cultural change is organizational climate, which is based on the perceptions of employees regarding work expectations, especially behaviours that are rewarded (Burke and Litwin, 1992). Creating an organizational climate that rewards and recognizes openness towards EBP can help facilitate cultural change in police organizations.

Fostering a climate of constructive dissent

Organizations often have a hard time listening to ideas that do not fit with their established beliefs and values; the key to countermanding this is creating an organization of constructive dissent. Most organizations discount new ideas, usually by countering with the argument of the way we have always done it is good enough. If someone brings forth a new idea that doesn't mesh with current thinking, no matter the logic or science behind it, it most likely will be discarded. 'You pay a price for dissent even when the issue is *hypothetical or inconsequential,*' Charlan Nemeth (2018: 203) warns us, 'You don't have to confront issues of national security to be punished for holding a minority opinion'. Sadly, nearly all of us punish dissent. We don't like disagreement with our beliefs, and we are very capable of inflicting punishment on those who oppose our views when we are in the majority. It is interesting that dissent is punished even when the issue is hypothetical or inconsequential. In policing, punishment most often comes in the form of cutting ties with a group or person or ostracizing them in the organization by moving them to a unit with little power.

Cultivating dissent strengthens the way we think and helps us to be more open in our thoughts and take our ideas in multiple directions (Nemeth, 2018). Without dissent, we fall into groupthink, which can lead to failed decisions. One way to cultivate dissent is to teach an organization how to critically think. Most individuals have not been taught how to think through a problem, how to examine their assumptions about a problem, to examine their information sources, and to examine the difference between correlation and causation. As part of her EBP course, Renée focuses on teaching how to critically think about policing issues. She reviews the biases we use to make assumptions about the world, with her primary question always being 'How do you know that?' She also advocates for organizations to stop allowing lazy thinking in their organization. When people make causal statements about correlating events, it has to be addressed immediately and not allowed in an evidence-based organization. When people make broad assumptions in department meetings, they need to be asked, 'How do you know that?' and they must be able to back up their statements with facts and data rather than opinion, feelings, or beliefs. Without thoughtful dissent, an organization will never grow. The majority opinion of the organization shapes how we think, and the result is poorer decisions and less creativity (Nemeth, 2018).

Post-mortem groups

Post-mortem groups are another way to slowly cultivate organizational shifts in thinking. Policing does not often review programs or policies to determine whether they were effective or efficient. Many programs are created in response to an incident that occurred in the police department, community pressure, or a national incident in policing that drives an organization to implement a new practice. These programs can run for years before a proper evaluation is completed – for example, the 'Scared Straight' program ran for over 20 years before an RCT was implemented and the program was discovered to have a backfire effect – the kids going through 'Scared Straight' committed more crime than those who didn't (Petrosino et al,

2013). Furthermore, many programs will experience mission drift and the initial goals of the program are no longer evaluated. For example, a program called Home for the Holidays was a traffic program designed to lower traffic fatalities in the city (Mitchell, 2017). It had been running for several years, and when the organization laid out the goals of the program – reducing traffic fatalities and the metrics they were capturing – traffic citations and warnings – the organization realized that the metrics they were gathering did not match the goals of the program.

Reviewing organizational programs on an annual basis is a way of doing a post-mortem that may revel whether the program is effective, efficient, creating harm, or at the very least, keeping the program on track with original goals. When teaching EBP to organizations Renée has executive management participate in a thought activity. She has them list out all the programs the organization engages in on the left side of a piece paper. Then she has them estimate the yearly cost of the program based on the number of hours officers dedicate to the program multiplied by an officer's average salary. She has them list out the organizational goals for the program and then the data they are compiling to determine if the program is effective. She asks them to determine if the goals they are attempting to achieve and the data they are gathering match. She asks if there is a comparison group. As Sherman states, 'The rock bottom standard for EBP is this: A comparison group is essential to every test to be included as "evidence" that a police decision causes a certain result' (2013: 420). And finally, she asks if they know whether their program is creating any harm for their communities, reminding them that without a rigorous evaluation, just like 'Scared Straight', without a comparison group, we may not know if we are creating harm (see below).

Killing your darlings

You must be willing to let go of programs and practices that are shown to be ineffective or inefficient, or, to put it in a not-so-light manner, you must 'kill your darlings' (Pittampali, 2016). We have seen this example in policing as services tenaciously hang

Evidence-based program evaluation

Programs	Cost	Goals	Statistics	Matching	Comparison	Harm
1						
2						
3						
4						

onto Drug Abuse Resistance Education (DARE), even though
the research keeps piling up demonstrating the ineffectiveness of
the program to prevent drug and alcohol use (West and O'Neal,
2004). It may be that agencies do not believe the research, or
it may be that police leaders want to appear consistent with
other decisions they have made (West and O'Neal, 2004).
Using DARE as an example, however, we know from direct
experience that in some instances it is frontline officers who are
huge supporters of this program. When pressed to explain why
in workshops or seminars, they reveal that it's because programs
like DARE provide 'out-of-the box' tools they can use with
little thought or pre-planning. In other words, they can be easy
to use, and convenience – especially within a busy operational
environment – shouldn't be dismissed too lightly.

The convenience issue raises an important point: it is very
difficult to convince people to 'kill their darlings' when they
are trying to fill a perceived or real need and do not have
accessible or suitable alternatives. One way to counter this is
to consider trialling other options. One of the smaller services
that Laura works with did this. Their school resource officers
felt they could develop a better program than DARE, and so
their chief agreed to bring in outside researchers to help them
test their new program against the version of DARE they had
been using (as well as against a 'control' school). Unfortunately,
we can't reveal the results, as the trial will not start until 2021.
However, we can report that developing the new program broke
the DARE spell and caused sufficient excitement that another
nearby police agency wants to import the new program and run
a similar trial. As you can see, a major benefit of being willing
to 'kill your darlings' is the opportunity to create initiatives that
might not only produce better outcomes, but also increase the
knowledge, experience, and morale of personnel.

Evidence-based policing ambassadors

EBP ambassadors, EBP champions, or, as they call them in the
New Zealand Police, EBP lead practitioners, are people in the
organization who understand EBP practices, who may have
had experience implementing research in their organization, are

committed to teaching others about EBP, and are attempting to embed EBP into the DNA of the organization. New Zealand Police Deputy Chief Executive Mark Evans (2019) describes their program as an attempt to 'facilitate EBP on the front line, influence staff who are apprehensive about the application and benefits of EBP and collect on-the-ground information and intelligence to improve EBP's continued implementation.'

Choosing an ambassador should be based on status in the organization rather than rank. In this sense, status refers not to one's position, but to the respect someone has earned within a group (Grant, 2016). Since the ambassador's primary job is to assist the organization in gaining a better understanding of EBP and they are attempting to shift someone's belief, trust matters most (Sharot, 2017). Trust is given more readily to people we are familiar with and who we see as having similar beliefs and values (Sharot, 2017). We are not alone in making this point. In discussing the need for selecting people with status, Peter Martin, a retired Deputy Commissioner from Western Australia Police Service, similarly suggests when identifying an 'EBP ambassador' finding people in the organization who have the trust and respect of the frontline officers, as these people are often the informal leaders in the organization. Use their influence to help build the organization's understanding of EBP.

Reducing resistance

Our own experiences of working to implement EBP in police services across two different continents have shown us there can be substantial resistance to adopting new models. While we have discussed some aspects of that resistance – largely in the form of the natural human inclination to prefer the status quo – there is another element that is equally important to address: change fatigue. One of us, Laura, has been in policing research for about 20 years. During that time, she has seen several different new approaches heralded as 'cures' for whatever appears to be ailing policing at that time. These include community policing (late 1980s, early 1990s), problem-oriented policing (early to mid-1990s), intelligence-led policing (mid-1990s), CompStat (mid-1990s), and then evidence-based policing (late 1990s to the present). This is a list of major models only and doesn't include each individual or regional initiative implemented by different police services, many of which were subsequently repealed and replaced five to ten years later when police executives changed. In a 30-year police career, that's a lot of change, and police employees are quite right to be sceptical that EBP is now going to be the latest 'cure'. Not only are we not advocating for that position; we don't think EBP advocates more generally should. Having a realistic, tempered view of what is and is not achievable will go a long way to reducing some internal resistance.

Something else that will likely help to reduce resistance is not to make immediate, wholesale changes or to impose EBP on those who might not be willing to engage. One of the police services with which Laura works has rolled out EBP in a staggered fashion, beginning with training frontline officers and some managers, and then rolling it out to those units that have people within who are eager to expand their current work and try something new. Even then, Laura, who works closely with this service, cautioned doing one or two small projects with key people in the unit, rather than trying to take on a unit-level project. Why? Small successes are easier to manage and allow individuals to model change and showcase 'what works' to their colleagues. Further, this approach gives people choice, and thus more of a sense of empowerment over their work environment, something that is often lacking when big 'cures' are rolled out on an institutional basis.

Summing up

In this chapter, we focused on ways to sustain evidence-based practices in an organization. We reviewed practical and holistic solutions in an attempt to give a broad overview of how to sustain change within an organization. We presented internal and external suggestions: to develop employees within the organization and partnerships outside the organization. Both approaches help to solidify the overall mission of the agency to advance evidence-based practices. Outside partnerships offer credibility to the organization by having an unbiased evaluation of current practices (Alpert et al, 2013). Building internal capacity allows the organization to build its own knowledge, skills, and abilities that can be handed down to future generations of officers, crime analysts, and executive management. We propose the use of internal and external efforts to support sustainability.

The practical solutions offered a good balance of internal and external support. First, look within, examine the workforce to see if there are employees with advanced degrees or specialized training who might contribute to the knowledge of the organization. If there is no intellectual capacity to be mined, then invest in the training to assist employees with understanding evidence-based practices. Purchase the required software or analytical tools needed. Invest in the people or areas that are needed to build sustainability. Create a culture of learning. Make sure employees are comfortable speaking up. Kill programs that are not working. Form post-mortem groups to examine what worked and what didn't. By examining programs using an evidence-based philosophy employees will begin to understand that learning is the true vision, that critical thinking takes a priority, rather than creating programs for the sake of appearing progressive.

Sustaining an evidence-based culture requires work. Agencies will have to make a concerted effort to reduce resistance from their employees, employing holistic and practical approaches along with internal and external efforts. This chapter presented suggestions to maintain an evidence-based culture after the early adopters have retired, been promoted, or left the organization. These solutions come from the officers, crime analysts, and executive managers who have worked in the field and examined the outcomes.

9

Resources for
evidence-based practices

Throughout this book we have looked at how to get started learning about evidence-based policing (EBP), whether you are an individual looking to educate yourself on the topic or a leader in a large organization attempting to shift cultural values, using agency size as a framework. Although we have used agency size as a framework, some large agencies (Chapter 7) might find solutions in the chapter on small agencies (Chapter 5) useful, and vice versa. That being the case, we thought a chapter dedicated entirely to useful evidence-based resources might be a handy go-to guide, no matter the size of the agency.

This chapter is broken down into various EBP Societies, policing organizations, and universities that have dedicated their resources to sharing evidence-based information.

We begin with the most obvious resources, the Societies of Evidence-Based Policing, and review some of what each of the Societies offers for their members.

Evidence-Based Policing Societies

UK Society of Evidence Based Policing (SEBP)

The first Society of Evidence Based Policing (SEBP) was formed in the UK, which is why their name and website does not indicate a country. At the time it was established, there were no similar societies. Because other countries soon followed suit and created similar societies, SEBP is referred to in the literature and in conferences as the UK Society of Evidence Based Policing, but on its website (see www.sebp.police.uk), its official name is the Society of Evidence Based Policing. It was founded in 2010 and is open 'to any member of police staff or researcher who is committed to making a positive impact in the community through using the best available research evidence', and is 'made up of police officers, police staff and research professionals who aim to make evidence based methodology part of everyday policing in the UK' (www.sebp.police.uk). You do not have to be a British citizen to be a member, and membership is free.

The goals of SEBP are:

- To increase the use of best available research evidence to solve police problems.
- To produce new research evidence by police practitioners and researchers.
- To communicate research evidence to police practitioners and the public.

It is easy to sign up for membership. With just an email address and a name, you will receive a reduced price to their annual conference, a reduced subscription to the *Journal of Experimental Criminology*, and the ability to network and learn from other practitioners. The *Journal of Experimental Criminology* is a wonderful resource for those interested in EBP, as it only publishes on experiments that meet Level 3 or above on the Maryland Scientific Methods Scale (SMS) (www.whatworksgrowth.org/resources/the-scientific-maryland-scale/), and many of the experiments are policing centric. Additionally, in the resource section of SEBP's website (www.sebp.police.uk/resources) there is a link to a PDF titled *How to be an Evidence Based Practitioner* written by David Harrington that explains how to think about applying research in an organization; it has a step-by-step chart that demonstrates how to evaluate the rigour of a particular research study. At the end of the guide there is a page that ranks resources for ease of understanding, which makes it a good resource for newcomers to EBP.

Australia & New Zealand Society of Evidence Based Policing (ANZSEBP)

The Australia & New Zealand Society of Evidence Based Policing (ANZSEBP) was established in 2013 in Brisbane, Australia, and is a police practitioner-led society (see www. anzsebp.com). Membership 'is open to any member of police staff or researcher who is committed to making a positive impact in the community through using the best available research evidence'. Full membership is for members living in New Zealand or Australia, and an associate membership is available for members outside these regions. ANZSEBP membership offerings are identical to those of the SEBP in the UK, except ANZSEBP membership offers a subscription to their *Police Science* journal published twice a year – a copy of the journal is emailed to you in PDF format once you become a member. The journal highlights the progress of all four respective EBP Societies across the world, and contains articles on a variety of EBP issues such as current research projects being conducted across the world, how to implement research in your own organization, and how to lead an organization to become evidence-based.

Canadian Society of Evidence-Based Policing (Can-SEBP)

The Canadian Society of Evidence-Based Policing (Can-SEBP) was formed in April 2015 by the co-author of this book, Dr Laura Huey (www.can-sebp.net/). It 'is an association of police practitioners, academic researchers, public policy-makers and others, whose mission is to foster the creation and mobilization of quality research in order to make evidence-based approaches a cornerstone of policing in Canada'; membership is free. The focus of Can-SEBP is to create tools for practitioners and academics that are useful and user-friendly. It has created resources that span every mode of learning, reading, listening, and watching. Can-SEBP produces a podcast hosted by Dr Huey that covers different topics in EBP, creates infographics on different types of studies – evaluating the strengths and weaknesses of the research designs – and records a video series on different types of research methods. Many of these tools can be accessed without being a member. For example, the Square 1 tool evaluates policing programs based against the current evidence to determine if there is any evidence to support the program (www.can-sebp.net/squareone).

The Square 1 tool is a rapid assessment approach. To assist their police practitioners in understanding the evidence base of a particular program, they answer five questions:

1. Is the program based on existing research?
2. Has the program been independently evaluated?
3. Was the program rigorously tested? (Level 4 or 5 on Ratcliffe's example at www.reducingcrime.com/post/ evidence-hierarchy or the Maryland SMS.)
4. Has the program evaluation been replicated or reproduced?
5. Was the program tested in Canada?

The Square 1 tool begins with a short overview of what the program is. For instance, Verbal Judo is explained as:

> Originally developed in the early 1980s by Dr George Thompson, Verbal Judo is a training program aimed at providing officers with various verbal skills that facilitate the successful resolution of situations and reduce the need for the use of force when possible. The skills and competencies taught in the program involve being professional, learning communication and deflection, developing an understanding of two different "contact models" that can be used to gain voluntary compliance, identifying when talking is not working and how to deal with that, and finally provides case studies and practice exercises to convey the material.

Answering question 2, reviewers determined that although the program claims it is based on psychological research, it is not evident what specific research it is based on. One evaluation was completed retroactively, and found that the officers felt as though their communication skills improved their de-escalation abilities, but the training did not lead to changes in use of force. The reviewers found no other evaluations and the program evaluation was never replicated. The Square 1 tool gives an overview of commonly implemented policing programs and allows readers to quickly understand the foundation of the evidence base and to determine whether the evaluation performed was a quality study.

In addition to the tools offered for non-members, members can gain access to another part of the website that has links to journal articles covering topics such as criminology, policing, and research methods. Clicking on the links will take you to a Google library created by Can-SEBP and some of the classic articles in criminology and policing.

American Society of Evidence-Based Policing (ASEBP)

The American Society of Evidence-Based Policing (ASEBP) is a practitioner-led society that was started in 2015 by a small group of police officers, including co-author Dr Renée J. Mitchell, and one crime analyst. Today it is run by active officers, retired officers, criminal justice activists, and researchers. The goal of ASEBP is similar to the other EBP Societies in that it tries to create use-friendly tools to inform its membership about current police research. ASEBP does this in mainly two ways – writing research briefs and running an annual conference (see www. AmericanSEBP.org).

The research briefs are two-page translations of research articles concerning topics that should be of interest to police officers. ASEBP focused on experiments that achieve a Level 4 or 5 on the Maryland SMS. The briefs are translated by graduate students and then reviewed by at least one of the original authors to ensure that the translations are neither too broad nor too narrow. This way, when the briefs are published, although they are condensed versions of the full research study, they are still accurate. They are only available to members, and ASEBP is the only policing society that charges for membership.

ASEBP also runs an in-person conference every spring. Due to the COVID-19 pandemic in 2020, ASEBP chose to switch to a virtual conference rather than cancelling. ASEBP hosted the conference for free, which led to 24 different countries attending the conference and over 1,000 attendees. Due to the large turn-out from countries all over the world, ASEBP decided to continue to host an annual virtual conference at the beginning of the year in addition to the in-person conference in the spring. The virtual conference can be viewed during the conference dates and the recorded sessions can be viewed up to two months afterwards. ASEBP recruits academics, practitioners, and pracademics who have conducted field research to present so the policing profession can be exposed to research they may find valuable. Its mission is to facilitate the use of research in policing, and by exposing police officers to field experiments, the hope is they will continue their exploration of EBP.

ASEBP is one of the smaller associations, with only 250 members, but it has built a wide network of people within the USA and internationally who advocate for EBP. ASEBP has found that although policing practices may be slightly different in other countries, the problems within countries that policing face are still the same – homelessness, drug addiction, opioid overdose, mental illness, and poverty.

By encouraging communication between academics and practitioners across countries, the hope is that in cooperation with Can-SEBP, ANZSEBP, and the original SEBP, the Societies can continue to grow and encourage the police to use and engage in EBP.

Policing organizations

There are policing organizations that have created evidence-based centres or research collaboratives within their organizations. These police agencies have prioritized understanding EBP and good research practices. Many have built their internal capacity through partnerships, education, and opening their doors to external researchers. By creating internal capacity, they have created resources for other police agencies to use and follow.

East Midlands Policing Academic Collaboration (EMPAC)

The East Midlands Policing Academic Collaboration (EMPAC) in the UK is a good example of building a large police/research coalition to educate police organizations and to build internal capacity to generate research. EMPAC is comprised of police and crime commissioners, five different police forces, and eight universities located near East Midlands Police Service. The aim of their collaboration is to embed research-informed problem-solving into East Midlands Police Service, to create knowledge exchange and transformation, and to inform policy and practice through the application of the evidence base. They state, 'The East Midlands Policing Academic Collaboration (EMPAC) is a cooperative network that combines the best of academic expertise and professional policing insight in a dynamic and exciting multilateral partnership that has a tangible impact on policing in the East Midlands and beyond'. Their website would be a good place to start if you are looking to create a coalition that resides within a police department (see www.empac.org. uk/about-empac/).

Scottish Institute for Policing Research (SIPR)

The Scottish Institute for Policing Research (SIPR) is another example of a large collaboration between a police service and a contingency of universities. The aim of Police Scotland and the 14 Scottish university partners is to 'carry out high quality, independent research and to make evidence-based contributions to policing policy and practice' (see www.sipr.ac.uk/). SIPR offers grants to fund small-scale research projects on policing issues. It awarded three grants in 2019 supporting research to evaluate investigative interviewing training, a facial composite system, and to create a kit for the collection of human DNA evidence in wildlife crime cases.

Active police officers in Scotland can apply to SIPR for a fellowship that can last from three months to a year. In order to apply, the officer must propose to test a policy or practice or have a desire to apply evidence-based policies to practice. During the fellowship, the officer will have the support of academics from the coalition to help them create the best research design to answer their question. The idea behind the fellowship is to assist the officer in developing an in-depth understanding of research so that when they go back to their organization, they are able to transfer their knowledge to their fellow officers. The fellowship offers a stipend to cover travel and some other small expenses. SIPR's website lists the officers and projects that have been selected for fellowship, but it does not list the outcomes or briefs of the projects' outcomes.

Like other policing coalitions, SIPR offers research briefs, conferences, and small stipends for field research. During the COVID-19 pandemic, SIPR collated the research they could find on policing pandemics and posted them on their website. SIPR offers local and international conferences on a variety of topics, with the most recent being a conference focused on cybersecurity. Additionally, they offer thematic networks focusing their research efforts on education and leadership, police–community relationships, evidence and education, and public protection. Each of these networks has a list of questions they are trying to answer with research. The networks were created to assist with the transfer of knowledge by creating a network of police practitioners and academics focused on a very specific area of policing.

New Zealand Evidence-Based Policing Centre (EBPC)

The New Zealand Evidence-Based Policing Centre (EBPC) is the only one of its kind in the world. Other large police agencies, like the Metropolitan Police, have a large research division, but no police agency has a centre dedicated entirely to the pursuit of EBP. The Centre does not approach policing problems in an entirely evidence-based framework; it also uses a crime science approach. This means that rather than try to evaluate all policing practices or programs using an experimental method, it will determine the research method based on the question posed. This could mean qualitative exploration if the question has never been posed before, or a retroactive look at a program conducted in a previous time period using pre or post data. The Centre focuses on practitioner-based research, research that will inform the practice of policing. These practitioner-focused studies help the New Zealand Police to implement measures to prevent crime and improve the allocation of police resources to better protect the public. The Centre offers research briefs on the studies they have conducted (see www.police. govt.nz/about-us/programmes-and-initiatives/evidence-based-policing-ebp/).

UK College of Policing

The UK College of Policing and the What Works Centre for Crime Reduction was formed in 2013 in response to the adoption of evidence-based practices across several different professions in the UK (the UK has a network of What Works Centres listed at www.gov.uk/guidance/what-works-network www.Gov.uk). The College of Policing was mentioned in Chapter 2, as we use their EBP definition to frame the book. The College of Policing is made up of academics and practitioners dedicated to informing police practice based on research. The What Works Centre (https://whatworks.college. police.uk/Pages/default.aspx/) has several useful tools: the Crime Reduction Toolkit (https://whatworks.college.police. uk/toolkit/Pages/Toolkit.aspx), the Evidence-Based Policing Maturity Model (https://whatworks.college.police.uk/Support/ Pages/maturity-model.aspx), the Cost Benefit Tool (https:// whatworks.college.police.uk/Research/Pages/Cost_Benefit_ Tool.aspx), the Policing Evaluation Toolkit (https://whatworks. college.police.uk/Support/Pages/Evaluation-Toolkit.aspx), and a Logic Model (https://whatworks.college.police.uk/Research/ Documents/LogicModel.pdf). These provide an advanced model of implementing or evaluating police practices against an evidence-based framework.

The Crime Reduction Toolkit is a user-friendly site that allows practitioners and academics to search for crime prevention interventions that are effective and efficient. It is a fantastic resource as the site allows the user to filter by how effective the intervention is, the problem the intervention is addressing, the focus of the intervention (prevention, diversion, or reoffending), the population (place-based, juvenile, adult), and intersecting factors (gangs, alcohol, drugs). It rates each intervention using the EMMIE framework.

EMMIE stands for:

- Effect: Was there an impact on crime?
- Mechanism: How did the intervention work? What was it about the intervention that can explain the effect?
- Moderators: Where does it work? In what circumstances will it work or not work?
- Implementation: How to implement it – what conditions are needed for it to work?
- Economic cost: How much does it cost to implement? Are there direct and indirect costs?

The tool is simple. Say you were looking for burglary prevention interventions that had a high likelihood of reducing burglaries. To use the toolkit, on the left-hand side of the page you would check the box 'works' under the impact section, 'prevention' in the focus section, and 'burglary' under the problem section. The first three interventions would be 'Alley gating', 'CCTV', and 'Hotspots policing'. Then, if you click on one of the topics, like the hotspots policing intervention, it will take you to the hotspots page explaining the intervention using the EMMIE framework, and at the end of the page it will give you an overall summary of the intervention, for example:

> Overall, the evidence suggests that hotspots policing has reduced crime. Hotspots policing programmes that take a problem-oriented approach appear more effective than increased traditional policing (eg increased patrols or enforcement). The evidence suggested that hotspots policing was more effective for drug offences, violent crime and disorder than it was for property crime. Hotspots policing can also lead to a diffusion of benefits to the areas immediately surrounding the hot spot. (https://whatworks. college.police.uk/toolkit/Pages/Intervention.aspx)

This website is really the best for ease of use, and understanding which crime prevention interventions work and which ones don't. You can go to this site without any instruction at all and figure out how to access the information you need without wasting time trying to navigate around the site.

The rest of the tools the What Works Centre offers are useful for assessing other aspects of interventions and to evaluate your agency. The Evidence-Based Policing Maturity Model, the Cost Benefit Toolkit, the Policing Evaluation Toolkit, and the Logic Model are each accompanied by a manual or tool that will take you step by step through applying the tool to practice. The Evidence-Based Policing Maturity Model tool can help evaluate where your police agency is at along a maturity continuum of evidence-based practices. As well as providing a manual to walk users through the model, a hard copy of the model is provided to write in and take notes, as well a virtual model where you can log all of your agency's progress online.

The Cost Benefit Tool contains information and guidance for practitioners who are new to evaluating interventions based on a cost benefit analysis. It contains a manual for evaluating interventions based on direct and indirect cost, titled *Economic Analysis: A Brief Guide for Crime Prevention Practitioners*, and several tools to assist you through the process.

The Policing Evaluation Toolkit helps police organizations evaluate their own interventions. Its intent is to help police agencies to understand if an intervention worked, how well it worked, and why it worked. Police agencies often seek outside parties to evaluate interventions, but this is often costly and time-consuming. Allocating some internal resources to understanding whether an intervention works or not will go a long way towards an agency becoming more effective and efficient.

The What Works Centre has also produced a how-to guide for creating a Logic Model. This is a method to critically think about the links between the problem at hand, the intervention, and the measures of success you are using. It is a visual template for understanding how and why you are implementing evidence-based practices. The What Works Centre has many useful tools that can be applied no matter where you are in relation to your understanding of EBP.

Universities

There are several universities that have centres dedicated to evidence-based practices or to policing research. These are just a small sample of universities that have tools that may be of assistance to new students of EBP.

Arizona State University, Tempe, USA

Arizona State University houses the Center for Problem-Oriented Policing (POP). The Center offers guides that are problem-, response-, or tool-specific (https://popcenter.asu.edu/pop-guides). Its approach to policing has not historically been evidence-based, as many police agencies left off the last 'A' of the SARA process for problem-solving – Scanning, Analysis, Response, and Assessment. The last part, Assessment, would be the evidence-based part, because an intervention can only be evidence-based if it was assessed using rigorous analytical methods. The Center is a good place to start for ideas about policing interventions, and the guides are well written and supported by research.

University of Michigan, Ann Arbor, USA

The University of Michigan houses the Inter-University Consortium for Political and Social Research (ICPSR). This Consortium maintains and provides access to a large archive of social science data. ICPSR also runs a summer program that provides short, intense training on advanced statistical methods. If an agency is interested in doing their own evaluations, they might think about sending an employee to a couple of the ICPSR courses (www.icpsr.umich.edu/web/pages/). An integral part of the infrastructure of social science research, ICPSR maintains and provides access to a vast archive of social science data for research and instruction.

George Mason University, Fairfax, USA

George Mason University houses the Center for Evidence-Based Crime Policy (CEBCP), whose mission is to make 'scientific research a key component in decisions about crime and justice policies' (www.cebcp.org). The Center offers several different resources – a free magazine twice a year titled *Translational Criminology*, a visual tool for categorizing research on police tactics called The Matrix, a technology page that hosts the current research on police technology, and one-page research briefs. Signing up for the *Translational Criminology* magazine is as easy as giving the University your email address. The magazine is typically filled with articles about current police research, thought-provoking opinion pieces, and ideas on where the future of police research should be headed. Academics, practitioners, and pracademics conducting their own research in their departments write the pieces contained within the magazine.

Veil of Darkness online tool

Racial bias has been an issue in policing for decades, but determining when it is occurring in a police department is difficult. Lori Fridell has written a guide titled *Understanding Race Data from Vehicle Stops: A Stakeholder's Guide*, published by the Police Executive Research Forum and the COPS Office (Fridell, 2005). In it, Fridell discusses the flaws in benchmarking used to determine disparity. The first one she points out is using population data and stops as a way to determine bias in policing. What she means is using the following comparisons: African Americans make up 18 percent of X police departments' traffic stops while African Americans only make up 8 percent of the city's population, from which it is concluded that X police department is engaging in racially biased traffic stops. If you review Fridell's guide, this is incorrect logic, and she gives a well-thought-out perspective on using traffic stops as an indicator of racial bias.

A better tool for police departments to determine if their department is engaging in racially biased stops is the Veil of Darkness tool created by RTI International, the RTI-STAR Traffic Stop Analysis Tool, which is free (www.rti.org/impact/rti-star-traffic-stop-analysis-tool). The tool 'uses a peer-reviewed, scientifically sound method to identify racial disproportionality ... this method is based on the assumption that police officers are less able to determine the race of a motorist when it is dark out.' Rather than looking at population disparity, the tool helps agencies analyse their stops based on the time of day they are occurring. RTI writes, 'Evidence of racial disproportionality exists if minority drivers are more likely to be stopped during the lighter periods of the inter-twilight period, compared to darker periods' (www.star.rti.org/). To use the tool, a police department just needs to have their traffic stop data in an Excel file that includes day or time of stop and race of driver. This tool can be helpful for an organization attempting to discern the level of racial disparity that is occurring within their police department.

Other associations and societies

Resources can be found with other associations that conduct research on issues that effect policing, such as the American Psychological Association (APA), the International Association of Crime Analysts (IACA), and the Global Law Enforcement and Public Health Association (GLEPHA). Membership is usually required for most of the associations, but some of them offer free resources. The APA recently posted a research brief reviewing a journal article, 'Policy and procedure recommendations for the collection and preservation of eyewitness identification evidence'. It has a page titled 'Science in Action' where you can find the research briefs (www.apa.org/action/). The IACA is a membership organization that provides a certification program for analysts, training courses, a yearly conference, and a new podcast titled *Analyst Talk*. The resources and course are all geared towards crime analysts, but as data is the foundation of EBP, having a membership in IACA could be a good counterpart to membership in one of the EBP Societies. GLEPHA is another association that provides resources for police officers. It is a not-for-profit, membership-based association whose mission is to promote research and understanding where the practice of public health and law enforcement intersect (www.gleapha. wildapricot.org).

Summing up

The resources available for individuals interested in EBP are growing. The IACA's podcast only started in June 2020, while Dr Jerry Ratcliffe's *Reducing Crime* podcast is in its 23rd episode. At the beginning of one of the author's explorations into EBP there was only one book that directly addressed the topic; now it seems at least one book a year is being published. Many of the tools Can-SEBP developed were only created over the last couple of years. ASEBP recently added a virtual conference that they plan to continue on a yearly basis. The UK College of Policing What Works Centre improves their online tools on a continual basis, and strives to add tools they view as integral to the support of practitioners in the field. More online tools are being created by societies, research institutes, and universities, and many are funded by the government every year.

This chapter has laid out the current resources available to those interested in EBP, but our hope is that within a year of publication there will be so many more than what we were able to review here.

Endnotes

Chapter 2

[1] COP can also be thought of as being comprised of four dimensions: philosophical, strategic, tactical, and organizational (Cordner and Scarborough, 2010).

[2] See Mastrofski (2019) for a thorough summary of these evidence reviews.

[3] This finding should not be surprising given that COP was originally implemented as a citizen-oriented cultural shift aimed at increasing police legitimacy and not as a crime reduction strategy.

Chapter 3

[1] There are many different variants of regression, some of which are suitable to use in experimental and quasi-experimental designs; however, for the purpose of this chapter, regression is referred to in its simplest form.

Chapter 4

[1] To be fair, while the police frequently get a bad rap for being conservative when it comes to adopting new ideas, they are hardly unique. Most humans suffer from what has been termed the 'status quo bias' – that is, a preference for maintaining an existing situation over something new (Kahnemann, 2013).

[2] In the UK, the College of Policing offers all members 'Athens' accounts, which provide access to academic literature. Elsewhere, as we describe in the next chapter, public libraries often offer similar access.

Chapter 6

[1] Some of the closest examples are Tasmania Police in Australia (approximately 1,200 sworn officers) and Bedfordshire Police in the UK (approximately 1,100 sworn officers).

References

Alpert, G.P., Rojek, J., and Hansen, J.A. (2013) *Building Bridges Between Police Researchers and Practitioners: Agents of Change in a Complex World*. Final Report to the National Institute of Justice, NCJ 244345. Available at: www.ncjrs.gov/pdffiles1/nij/grants/244345.pdf

Altman, N. and Krzywinski, M. (2015) 'Points of significance: Simple linear regression', *Nature Methods*, 12(11), 999–1000. Available at: https://doi.org/10.1038/nmeth.3627

Andresen, M. and Malleson, N. (2014) 'Police foot patrol and crime displacement: A local analysis', *Journal of Contemporary Criminal Justice*, 30(2): 186–99.

Ariel, B., Farrar, W.A., and Sutherland, A. (2015) 'The effect of police body-worn cameras on use of force and citizens' complaints against the police: A randomized controlled trial', *Journal of Quantitative Criminology*, 31(3): 509–35.

Ariel, B., Lawes, D., Weinborn, C., Henry, R., Chen, K., and Sabo, H. (2019) 'The "less-than-lethal weapons effect" – Introducing TASERs to routine police operations in England and Wales: A randomized controlled trial', *Criminal Justice and Behavior*, 46(2): 280–300. doi:10.1177/0093854818812918.

Ariel, B., Sutherland, A., Henstock, D., Young, J., et al (2016) 'Wearing body cameras increases assaults against officers and does not reduce police use of force: Results from a global multi-site experiment', *European Journal of Criminology*, 13(6), 744–755.

Arksey, H. and O'Malley, L. (2005) 'Scoping studies: Towards a methodological framework', *International Journal of Social Research Methodology: Theory & Practice*, 8(1), 19–32. Available at: https://doi.org/10.1080/1364557032000119616

Barker, E. (2017) *Barking up the Wrong Tree: The Surprising Science Behind Why Everything You Know About Success Is (Mostly) Wrong*, New York: Harper.

Bayley, D.H. (1994) *Police for the Future*, New York: Oxford University Press.

Belkhodja, O., Amara, N., Landry, R., and Ouimet, M. (2007) 'The extent and organizational determinants of research utilization in Canadian health services organizations', *Science Communication*, 28(3): 377–417.

Bennett, S., Newman, M., and Sydes, M. (2017) 'Mobile police community office: A vehicle for reducing crime, crime harm and enhancing police legitimacy?', *Journal of Experimental Criminology*, 13: 417–28. doi:10.1007/s11292-017-9302-6.

Bierly, P.E. III, Damanpour, F. and Santoro, M.D. (2009) 'The application of external knowledge: Organizational conditions for exploration and exploitation', *Journal of Management Studies*, 46(3), 481–509.

Blaskovits, B., Bennell, C., Huey, L., Kalyal, H., Walker, T., and Javela, S. (2018) 'A Canadian replication of Telep and Lum's (2014) Examination of police officers' receptivity to empirical research', *Policing & Society*. Available at: https://doi.org/10.1080/10439463.2018.1522315

Bottema, A. and Telep, C. (2019) 'The benefit of intelligence officers: Assessing their contributions to success through actionable intelligence', *Policing: An International Journal*, 42(1): 2–15.

Bowers, K. and Johnson, S. (2005) 'Domestic burglary repeats and space-time clusters: The dimensions of risk', *European Journal of Criminology*, 2(1): 67–92.

Bradley, D. and Nixon, C. (2009) 'Ending the "Dialogue of the Deaf": Evidence and policing policies and practices. An Australian case study', *Police Practice and Research*, 10(5–6): 423–35.

Braga, A. (2013) 'Embedded criminologists in police departments', *Ideas in American Policing*, 17: 1–19.

Braga, A. and Davis, E. (2014) 'Implementing science in police agencies: The embedded research model', Policing: A Journal of Policy and Practice, 8(4): 294–306.

Braga, A. and MacDonald, J. (2019) 'Improving police effectiveness in ensuring justice', *Criminology & Public Policy*, 18(3): 511–23.

Braga, A. and Schnell, C. (2013) 'Evaluating place-based policing strategies: Lessons learned from the Smart Policing Initiative in Boston', *Police Quarterly*, 16(3): 339–57.

Braga, A.A. and Weisburd, D. (2010) *Policing Problem Places: Crime Hot Spots and Effective Prevention*, New York: Oxford University Press.

Braga, A., Papachristos, A., and Hureau, D. (2014a) 'The effects of hot spots policing on crime: An updated systematic review and meta-analysis', *Justice Quarterly*, 31(4): 633–63.

Braga, A., Welsh, B., and Schnell, C. (2015) 'Can policing disorder reduce crime? A systematic review and meta-analysis', *Journal of Research in Crime & Delinquency*, 52(4): 567–88.

Braga, A., Welsh, B., and Schnell, C. (2019a) 'Disorder policing to reduce crime: A systematic review', *Campbell Systematic Reviews*, 15(3).

Braga, A.A., Turchan, B.S., Papachristos, A.V. and Hureau, D.M. (2019b) 'Hot spots policing and crime reduction: An update of an ongoing systematic review and meta-analysis', *Journal of Experimental Criminology*, 15(3), 289–311. Available at: https://doi.org/10.1007/s11292-019-09372-3

Braga, A.A., Welsh, B.C., Papachristos, A.V., Schnell, C., and Grossman, L. (2014b) 'The growth of randomized experiments in policing: The vital few and the salience of mentoring', *Journal of Experimental Criminology*, 10(1), 1–28.

Bratton, W. and Malinowski, S. (2008) 'Police performance management in practice: Taking CompStat to the next level', *Policing*, 2(2): 259–65.

Brimicombe, A. (2016) 'Analysing police-recorded data', *Legal Information Management*, 16(2): 71–7.

Brown, J., McDowall, A., Gamblin, D., and Fenn, L. (2018) 'Assessing transmission and translation of learning about evidence based policing by graduate trainee police officers', *Policing: A Journal of Policy and Practice*, 14(1): 119–34. Available at: https://doi.org/10.1093/police/pay072

Brubacher, J., Chan, H., Brasher, P., Erdelyi, S., et al (2014) 'Reduction in fatalities, ambulance calls, and hospital admissions for road trauma after implementation of new traffic laws', *American Journal of Public Health*, 104(1): e89–e97.

Bullock, K. and Tilley, N. (2009) 'Evidence based policing and crime reduction', *Policing*, 3(4): 381–87.

Burke, W. and Litwin, G. (1992) 'A causal model of organization performance and change', *Journal of Management*, 18(3): 523–45.

Carter D.L. and Carter J.G. (2009) 'Intelligence-led policing: Conceptual and functional considerations for public policy', *Criminal Justice Policy Review*, 20(3), 310–25.

Carter, J. (2016) 'Institutional pressures and isomorphism: The impact on intelligence-led policing adoption', *Police Quarterly*, 19(4): 435–60.

Chan, J. (1997) *Changing Police Culture: Policing in a Multicultural Society*, Cambridge: Cambridge University Press.

Clary, K. (2019) Notes from the field: Evidence-based practice – Employing evidence to combat everyday tragedy', National Institute of Justice. Available at: https://nij.ojp.gov/topics/articles/notes-field-evidence-based-practice-employing-evidence-combat-everyday-tragedy

Clearfield, C. and Tilcsik, A. (2018) *Meltdown: What Plane Crashes, Oil Spills, and Dumb Business Decisions Can Teach Us About How to Succeed at Work and at Home*, London: Penguin.

Cockbain, E. and Knutsson, J. (2015) *Applied Police Research: Challenges and Opportunities*, Abingdon: Routledge.

College of Policing (2018) 'What is evidence-based policing?' Available at: https://whatworks.college.police.uk/About/Pages/What-is-EBP.aspx

College of Policing (2019a) *Crime Reduction Toolkit*. Available at: https://whatworks.college.police.uk/toolkit/Pages/Welcome.aspx

College of Policing (2019b) 'Policing Education Qualifications Framework (PEQF).' Available at: www.college.police.uk/What-we-do/Learning/Policing-Education-Qualifications-Framework/Pages/Policing-Education-Qualifications-Framework.aspx

COPS Office (2019) *The Beat*, US Department of Justice. Available at: https://cops.usdoj.gov/thebeat

Cordner, G. (2018) 'A Practical Approach to Evidence Based Policing', in R.J. Mitchell and L. Huey (eds) *Evidence Based Policing: An Introduction*, Bristol: Policy Press, 231–42.

Cordner, G. and Scarborough, K.E. (2010) *Police Administration*, 7th edition, Amsterdam: Elsevier.

Corsaro, N., Hunt, E., Ipple, N., and McGarrell, E. (2012) 'The impact of drug market pulling levers policing on neighborhood violence', *Criminology & Public Policy*, 11(2): 167–99.

Coyle, D. (2017) *The Culture Code: The Secrets of Highly Successful Groups*, New York: Random House.

Crawford, A. (2009) *Situating Anti-Social Behaviour and Respect*, Leeds: CCJS Press. Available at: http://eprints.whiterose.ac.uk/43591/

Darroch, S. and Mazerolle, L. (2013) 'Intelligence-led policing: A comparative analysis of organizational factors influencing innovation uptake', *Police Quarterly*, 16(1): 3–37.

Drawve, G., Bleongie, M., and Steinman, H. (2017) 'The role of crime analyst and researcher partnerships: A training exercise in Green Bay, Wisconsin', *Policing*, 12(3): 277–87.

Drezner, D. (2017) *The Ideas Industry: How Pessimists, Partisans, and Plutocrats Are Transforming the Marketplace of Ideas*, Oxford: Oxford University Press.

Drover, P. and Ariel, B. (2015) 'Leading an experiment in police body-worn video cameras', *International Criminal Justice Review*, 25(1): 80–97.

Dupont, B. (2004) 'Security in the age of networks', *Policing and Society*, 14(1), 76–91.

Dyer, J.M. and Dyer, F.C. (1965) *Bureaucracy Vs Creativity*, Coral Gables, FL: University of Miami Press.

Eck, J. (2019) 'Advocate: Why Problem-oriented Policing', In D. Weisburd and A.A. Braga (eds) *Police Innovation: Contrasting Perspectives* (2nd edn), Cambridge: Cambridge University Press, 165–81.

Eck, J. and Spelman, W. (1987) 'Problem solving: Problem-oriented policing in Newport News', *Police Executive Research Forum*.

Engel, R. (2005) 'Citizens' perceptions of distributive and procedural injustice during traffic stops with police', *Journal of Research in Crime & Delinquency*, 42(4): 445–81.

Eterno, J. and Silverman, E. (2012) *The Crime Numbers Game: Management by Manipulation*, Boca Raton, FL: CRC Press.

Evans, M. (2019) 'Leading the way in evidence-based policing', New Zealand Police, June. Available at: www.police.govt. nz/news/ten-one-magazine/leading-way-evidence-based-policing

Farrington, D.P., Gottfredson, D.C., Sherman, L.W., and Welsh, B.C. (2002) 'Maryland Scientific Methods Scale', in D. Farrington, D. MacKenzie, L. Sherman and B. Welsh (eds) *Evidence-Based Crime Prevention*, London: Routledge. Available at: https://doi.org/10.4324/9780203166697

Ferguson, L. (2019) 'A beginner's guide to critically consuming research.' Available at: www.can-sebp.net

Finnegan, H.A., Timmons Fritz, P.A., and Horrobin, B. (2018) 'Differential effects of gender on Canadian police officers' perceptions of stalking', *Criminal Justice and Behavior*, 45(4), 468–82.

Fleming, J. and Wingrove, J. (2017) '"We would if we could ... but not sure if we can": Implementing evidence-based practice: The evidence-based practice agenda in the UK', *Policing: A Journal of Policy and Practice*, 11(2): 202–13.

Fowler, F.J. (2013) *Survey Research Methods* (5th edn), Thousand Oaks, CA: Sage Publications.

Fragale, A., Overbeck, J., and Neale, M. (2011) 'Resources versus respect: Social judgments based on targets' power and status positions', *Journal of Experimental Social Psychology*, 47(4): 767–75.

Fridell, L.A. (2005) *Understanding Race Data from Vehicle Stops: A Stakeholder's Guide*, Washington, DC: Police Executive Research Forum.

Frisch, N. (2016) 'Examining the success of an embedded criminologist partnership', *Translational Criminology*, Spring, 24–6.

Giacomantonio, C., Goodwin, S., and Carmichael, G. (2019) 'Learning to de-escalate: Evaluating the behavioural impact of verbal Judo training on police constables', *Police Practice and Research*. doi:10.1080/15614263.2019.1589472.

Gibson, C., Slothower, M., and Sherman, L.W. (2017) 'Sweet spot for hot spots? A cost-effective comparison of two patrol strategies', *Cambridge Journal of Evidence Based Policing*, 1: 225. Available at: https://doi.org/10.1007/s41887-017-0017-8

Gill, C., Weisburd, D., Telep, C.W., Vitter, Z., and Bennett, T. (2014) 'Community-oriented policing to reduce crime, disorder and fear and increase satisfaction and legitimacy among citizens: A systematic review', *Journal of Experimental Criminology*, 10(4): 399–428.

Gladwell, M. (2000) *The Tipping Point*, New York: Little, Brown & Co.

Goldstein, H. (1987) 'Toward community-oriented policing: Potential, basic requirements, and threshold questions', *Crime & Delinquency*, 33(1): 6–30.

Goldstein, H. (2001) 'Problem-Oriented Policing in a Nutshell', Paper presented at the International Problem-Oriented Policing Conference, San Diego, CA. Available at: https://popcenter. asu.edu/content/key-elements-problem-oriented-policing-0

Goodison, S. and Wilson, T. (2017) *Citizen Perceptions of Body-Worn Cameras: A Randomized Controlled Trial*, Washington, DC: Police Executive Research Forum. Available at: https:// perf.memberclicks.net/assets/bodyworncameraperceptions.pdf

Grant, A. (2013) *Give and Take: Why Helping Others Drives Success*, New York: Viking.

Grant, A. (2016) *Originals: How Non-Conformists Move the World*, New York: Penguin Books.

Green, E. and Rossler, M.T. (2019) 'Examining job satisfaction among analysts: the impact of departmental integration, role clarity, and it responsibilities', *International Journal of Police Science & Management*, 21(2), 108–15. doi:10.1177/1461355719844278

Groff, E., Ratcliffe, J., Haberman, C., Sorg, E., Joyce, N., and Taylor, R. (2015) 'Does what police do at hot spots matter? The Philadelphia Policing Tactics Experiment', *Criminology*, 53(1): 23–53.

Hammersley, M. and Atkinson, P. (2007) *Ethnography: Principles in Practice* (3rd edn), London: Routledge.

Hashimi, S., Bouchard, M., and Morselli, C. (2016) 'A method to detect criminal networks from police data', *Methodological Innovations*, 9: 1–14.

Heaton, R. and Tong, S. (2016) 'Evidence based policing: From effectiveness to cost-effectiveness', *Policing*, 10(1): 60–70.

Hesse-Biber, S. and Leavy, P. (2011) *The Practice of Qualitative Research* (2nd edn), Thousand Oaks, CA: Sage Publications.

Hox, J. and Boeije, R.H. (2005) 'Data collection primary vs secondary', *Encyclopedia of Social Measurement*, Volume 1, Elsevier Inc.

Huey, L. (2016) *What One Might Expect: A Scoping Review of the Canadian Policing Research Literature*, Sociology Publications, 36.

Huey, L. and Bennell, C. (2017) 'Replication and reproduction in Canadian policing research: A note', *Canadian Journal of Criminology and Criminal Justice*, 59(1). doi:10.3138/cjccj.2016.E09

Huey, L. and Koziarski, J. (in review) 'The irrationalities of rationality in police data processes', *British Journal of Criminology*.

Huey, L., Kalyal, H., Peladeau, H., and Lindsay, F. (2018b) '"If you're gonna make a decision, you should understand the rationale": Is post-graduate education preparing Canadian police leaders for evidence based policing?', *Policing, a Journal of Policy and Practice*. Available at: https://doi.org/10.1093/police/pay086

Huey, L., Blaskovits, B., Bennell, C., Kalyal, H., and Walker, T. (2017) 'To what extent do Canadian police professionals believe that their agencies are "targeting, testing, and tracking" new policing strategies and programs?', *Police Practice and Research*, 18(6): 544–55.

Huey, L., Blaskovits, B., Bennell, C., Kalyal, H., and Walker, T. (2018a) 'Identifying Some Misconceptions about Evidence Based Policing: A Research Note', in R.J. Mitchell and L. Huey (eds) *Evidence Based Policing: An Introduction*, Bristol: Policy Press, 51–62.

IACP (International Association of Chiefs of Police) (2014) *Midsize Police Agencies: Surviving, Thriving, and Forging a New Business Model for Law Enforcement in a Post-Recession Economy*, Washington, DC: Office of Community Oriented Policing Services. Available at: www.theiacp.org/sites/default/files/2018-09/MSA_Success_In_Post-Recession_Economy.pdf

ICPSR (Inter-University Consortium for Political and Social Research) (2019) 'Summer Program in Quantitative Methods of Social Research.' Available at: www.icpsr.umich.edu/web/pages/sumprog/

Innes, M., Fielding, N., and Cope, N. (2005) '"The appliance of science?" The theory and practice of crime intelligence analysis', *British Journal of Criminology*, 45: 39–57.

Isaacson, W. (2011) *Steve Jobs*, New York: Simon & Schuster.

Johnson, S.D., Tilley, N., and Bowers, K. (2015) 'Introducing EMMIE: An evidence rating scale to encourage mixed-method crime prevention synthesis reviews', *Journal of Experimental Criminology*, 11(4): 459–73.

Johnson, S.D., Davies, T., Murray, A., Ditta, P., Belur, J., and Bowers, K. (2017) 'Evaluation of Operation Swordfish: A near-repeat target-hardening strategy', *Journal of Experimental Criminology*, 13, 505–25. Available at: https://doi.org/10.1007/s11292-017-9301-7

Justice Clearinghouse (2019) 'Upcoming webinars'. Available at: www.justiceclearinghouse.com/calendar-page/

Kahnemann, D. (2013) *Thinking Fast and Slow*, New York: Farrar, Strauss & Giroux.

Kalyal, H. (2019) '"Well, there's a more scientific way to do it!": Factors influencing receptivity to evidence-based practices in police organizations', *Police Practice and Research: An International Journal*. Available at: https://doi.org/10.1080/15614263.2019.1608548

Kalyal, H., Huey, L., Blaskovits, B., and Bennell, C. (2018) '"If it's not worth doing half-assed, then it's not worth doing at all": Police views as to why new strategy implementation fails', *Police Practice and Research: An International Journal*. doi:10.1080/15614263.2018.1526687.

Kaplan, W. (2017) *Why Dissent Matters: Because Some People See Things the Rest of Us Miss*, Montreal: McGill-Queen's University Press.

Keay, S. and Kirby, S. (2018) 'The evolution of the police analyst and the influence of evidence-based policing', *Policing*, 12(3): 265–76.

Knopper, S. (2013) 'iTunes' 10th anniversary: How Steve Jobs turned the industry upside down', *Rolling Stone*. Available at: www.rollingstone.com/culture/culture-news/itunes-10th-anniversary-how-steve-jobs-turned-the-industry-upside-down-68985/

Knutsson, J. and Tompson, L. (eds) (2017) *Advances in Evidence-Based Policing*, London: Taylor & Francis.

Lee, R.M. (1993) *Doing Research on Sensitive Topics*. Thousand Oaks, CA: Sage Publications.

Lofland, J., Snow, D.A., Anderson, L., and Lofland, L.H. (2006) *Analyzing Social Settings. A Guide to Qualitative Observation and Analysis 4*, Belmont, CA: Wadsworth/Thomson Learning.

Loftus, B. (2010) 'Police occupational culture: Classic themes, altered times', *Policing & Society*, 20(1): 1–20.

Lum, C. (2009) *Translating Police Research into Practice*, Ideas in American Policing, Washington, DC: National Police Foundation.

Lum, C. and Koper, C. (2017) *Evidence-Based Policing: Translating Research into Practice*, Oxford: Oxford University Press.

Lum, C., Koper, C., and Telep, C.W. (2011) 'The evidence-based policing matrix', *Journal of Experimental Criminology*, 7(1): 3–26.

Lum, C., Telep, C.W., Koper, C., and Grieco, J. (2012) 'Receptivity to research in policing', *Justice Research and Policy*, 14, 61–95.

Macbeth, E. and Ariel, B. (2019) 'Place-based statistical versus clinical predictions of crime hot spots and harm locations in Northern Ireland', *Justice Quarterly*, 36(1): 93–126.

Madensen, T. and Sousa, W. (2015) 'Practical Academics: Positive Outcomes of Police–Researcher Collaborations', in E. Cockbain and J. Knutsson (eds) *Applied Police Research: Challenges and Opportunities*, Abingdon: Routledge, 68–81.

Magnusson, M. (2018) 'Bridging the gaps by including the police officer perspective? A study of the design and implementation of an RCT in police practice and the impact of pracademic knowledge', *Policing: A Journal of Policy and Practice*, 14(2): 438–55. Available at: https://doi.org/10.1093/police/pay022

Manning, P. (2014) 'Ethnographies of the Police', in M. Reisig and R. Kane (eds) *The Oxford Handbook of Police and Policing*, New York: Oxford University Press, 518–47.

Mark, A., Whitford, A., and Huey, L. (2019) 'What does robbery really cost? An exploratory study into calculating costs and "hidden costs" of policing opioid-related robbery offences', *International Journal of Police Science and Management*, 21(2): 116–29.

Martin, P. (2018) 'Moving to the Inevitability of Evidence Based Policing', in R.J. Mitchell and L. Huey (eds) *Evidence Based Policing: An Introduction*, Bristol: Policy Press, 199–213.

Martin, P. and Mazerolle, L. (2016) 'Police leadership in fostering evidence-based agency reform', *Policing: A Journal of Policy and Practice*, 10(1): 34–43.

Maslow, A. (1966) *The Psychology of Science*, New York: Joanna Cotler Books.

Mastrofski, S. (2019) 'Critic: Community Policing: A Sceptical View', in D. Weisburd and A. Braga (eds) *Police Innovation: Contrasting Perspectives* (2nd edn), Cambridge: Cambridge University Press, 45–68.

Mastrofski, S.D. and Willis, J.J. (2010) 'Police organization continuity and change: Into the twenty-first century', *Crime and Justice*, 39(1): 55–144.

Mazerolle, L., Bennett, S., Davis, J., Sargent, E., and Manning, M. (2013) 'Procedural justice and police legitimacy: A systematic review of the research evidence', *Journal of Experimental Criminology*, 9(3): 245–74.

McCord, J. (2003) 'Cures that harm: Unanticipated outcomes of crime prevention programs', *The Annals of the American Academy of Political and Social Science*, 587(1): 16–30.

Miley, L. and Shreve, T. (2019) *Crimeversation*. Available at: https://player.fm/series/crimeversation

Mitchell, R.J. (2017) *Evidence-Based Policing*, Grand Prairie, TX: Grand Prairie Police Department.

Mitchell, R.J. and Huey, L. (eds) (2018) *Evidence Based Policing: An Introduction*, Bristol: Policy Press.

Mitchell, R.J. and Lewis, S. (2017) 'Intention is not method, belief is not evidence, rank is not proof: Ethical policing needs evidence-based decision making', *International Journal of Emergency Services*, 6(3): 188–99.

Mitchell, R.J., Telep, C., and Lum, C. (2017) *The Ten-Step Guide for Conducting In-House Experimental Evaluations*, Fairfax, VA: Center for Evidence-Based Crime Policy, George Mason University.

Moore, M. (2003) 'Sizing up CompStat: An important administrative innovation in policing', *Criminology & Public Policy*, 2(3): 469–94.

Moore, G. (2014) *Crossing the Chasm: Marketing and Selling Disruptive Products to Mainstream Customers* (3rd edn), New York: HarperCollins.

Morgan, D.L. (2004) 'Focus groups', in S.N. Hesse-Biber and P. Leavy (eds) *Approaches to Qualitative Research*, New York : Oxford University Press, 263–85.

Morse, J.M., Barrett, M., Mayan, M., Olson, K., and Spiers, J. (2002) 'Verification strategies for establishing reliability and validity in qualitative research', *International Journal of Qualitative Methods*, 1, 1–19. Available at: www.ualberta.ca/~ijqm/

Moskos, P. and Taylor, L. (2019) *Quality Policing*, Podcast. Available at: https://qualitypolicing.com/about/

Mosiman, D. (2018) 'Violence reduction initiative relies on police community outreach, extra enforcement', *Wisconsin State Journal*, July 9.

Murray, A. (2018) 'Why Is Evidence Based Policing Growing and What Challenges Lie Ahead?', in R.J. Mitchell and L. Huey (eds) *Evidence Based Policing: An Introduction*, Bristol: Policy Press, 215–29.

National Institute of Justice (2019) *Criminal Justice Research*, Podcasts. Available at: https://podcasts.apple.com/us/podcast/criminal-justice-research-podcasts-from-national-institute/id458089139

Nawaz, A. and Tankebe, J. (2018) 'Tracking procedural justice in stop and search encounters: Coding evidence from body-worn video cameras', *Cambridge Journal of Evidence Based Policing*, 2: 139–63. Available at: https://doi.org/10.1007/s41887-018-0029-z

Nemeth, C. (2018) *In Defense of Troublemakers: The Power of Dissent in Life and Business*, New York: Basic Books.

Neyroud, P. (2015) 'Evidence-based triage in prosecuting arrestees: Testing an actuarial system of selective targeting', *International Criminal Justice Review*, 25(1): 117–31.

Nisbett, R. (2015) *Mindware: Tools for Smart Thinking in 2015*, New York: Farrar, Strauss, & Giroux.

Oswald, M., Grace, J., Urwin, S., and Barnes, G.C. (2018) 'Algorithmic risk assessment policing models: Lessons from the Durham HART model and "Experimental" proportionality', *Information & Communications Technology Law*, 27(2), 223–50, doi:10.1080/13600834.2018.1458455

Paoline, E. (2014) 'Police Culture', in G. Bruinsma and D. Weisburd (eds) *Encyclopedia of Criminology and Criminal Justice*, New York: Springer, 3577–86.

Pegram, R. (2018) 'Introduction to evidence-based policing.' Presentation at the Crime Prevention in Policing: What works? Seminar, December 4, London: Houses of Parliament, Westminster.

Pegram, R., Barnes, G.C., Slothower, M., and Strang, H. (2018) 'Implementing a burglary prevention program with evidence-based tracking', *Cambridge Journal of Evidence Based Policing*, 2(3–4): 181–91. Available at: https://doi.org/10.1007/s41887-018-0030-6

Petrosino, A., Turpin-Petrosino, C., Hollis-Peel, M.E., and Lavenberg, J.G. (2013) '"Scared Straight" and other juvenile awareness programs for preventing juvenile delinquency', *The Cochrane Database of Systematic Reviews*, April 30, 4. Available at: https://pubmed.ncbi.nlm.nih.gov/23862186/

Piza, E. and Feng, S. (2017) 'The current and potential role of crime analysts in evaluations of police interventions: Results from a survey of the International Association of Crime Analysts', *Police Quarterly*, 20(4): 339–66.

Pittampali, A. (2016) *Persuadable*, New York: HarperCollins.

Planck, M. (1949) *Scientific Autobiography: And Other Papers*, Open Road Media.

Potts, J. (2018) 'Research in brief: Assessing the effectiveness of automatic license plate readers', *The Police Chief*. Available at: www.theiacp.org/sites/default/files/2018-08/March%20 2018%20RIB.pdf

Ratcliffe, J. (2008) *Intelligence-Led Policing*, Cullompton: Willan Publishing.

Ratcliffe, J. (2016) *Intelligence-Led Policing* (2nd edn), New York: Routledge.

Ratcliffe, J. (2018a) *Reducing Crime: A Companion for Police Leaders*, London: Routledge.

Ratcliffe, J. (2018b) *Reducing Crime*, March, Podcast. Available at: www.reducingcrime.com/podcast

Ratcliffe, J. (2020) 'Evidence hierarchy', *Reducing Crime*, August 23. Available at: www.reducingcrime.com/post/evidence-hierarchy

Ratcliffe, J. and Rengert, G. (2008) 'Near repeat patterns in Philadelphia shootings', *Security Journal*, 21(1–2): 58–76.

Ratcliffe, J. and Sorg, E. (2017) *Foot Patrol: Rethinking the Cornerstone of Policing*, Cham, Switzerland: Springer.

Ratcliffe, J., Taniguchi, T., Groff, E., and Wood, J. (2011) 'The Philadelphia foot patrol experiment: A randomized controlled trial of police patrol effectiveness in violent crime hotspots', *Criminology*, 49(3): 795–831.

Ratcliffe, J., Taylor, R., Askey, A., Thomas, K., et al (2020) 'The Philadelphia predictive policing experiment', *Journal of Experimental Criminology*. Available at: https://doi.org/10.1007/s11292-019-09400-2

Reaves, B.A. (2015) 'Local police departments, 2013: Personnel, policies, and practices', Bulletin, NCJ 248677, US Department of Justice, Office of Justice Programs. Available at: www.bjs.gov/content/pub/pdf/lpd13ppp.pdf

Reichers, A.E., Wanous, J.P., and Austin, J.T. (1997) 'Understanding and managing cynicism about organizational change', *Academy of Management Executive*, 11: 48–59.

Reuss-Ianni, E. (1983) *Two Cultures of Policing: Street Cops and Management Cops*, New Brunswick, NJ: Transaction Books.

Riley County Police Department (2020) 'Initiative: Laser Point – RCPD's Intelligence-Led Policing Effort.' Available at: www.rileycountypolice.org/programs-services/rcpd-specialized-unitsprograms/initiative-laser-point-rcpds-intelligence-led

Roche, G. (1979) 'Much ado about mentors', *Harvard Business Review*, January.

Roeder, O.K., Eisen, L.-B.,Bowling, J.,Stiglitz, J.E., and Chettiar, I.M. (2015) *What Caused the Crime Decline?*, Columbia Business School Research Paper No 15-28. Available at https://ssrn.com/abstract=2566965 or http://dx.doi.org/10.2139/ssrn.2566965

Rogers, E.M. (1962) *Diffusion of Innovations*, New York: Free Press of Glencoe.

Rogers, E.M. (2010) *Diffusion of Innovations* (4th edn), New York: Simon & Schuster.

Salkind, N.J. (2010) *Encyclopaedia of Research Design*, Thousand Oaks, CA: SAGE Publications.

Sampson, R. and Raudenbush, S.W. (1999) 'Systematic social observation of public spaces: A new look at disorder in urban neighborhoods', *American Journal of Sociology*, 105(3), 603–51.

Santos, R. (2014) 'The effectiveness of crime analysis for crime reduction: Cure or diagnosis?', *Journal of Contemporary Criminal Justice*, 30(2): 147–68.

Santos, R. (2017) 'Police organizational change after implementing crime analysis and evidence-based strategies through stratified policing', *Policing*, 12(3): 288–302.

Saulnier, A. (2019) 'The effect of body-worn cameras on public perceptions of police: A Canadian study', *Blue Line*. Available at: www.blueline.ca/the-effect-of-body-worn-cameras-on-public-perceptions-of-police-a-canadian-study-6341/

Schein, E.H. (1988) *Organizational Culture and Leadership: A Dynamic View*, San Francisco, CA: Jossey-Bass Publishers.

Schlender, B. and Tetzeli, R. (2015) *Becoming Steve Jobs: The Evolution of a Reckless Upstart into a Visionary Leader*, New York: Crown.

Seale, C. (1999) *Introducing Qualitative Methods: The Quality of Qualitative Research*, London: Sage Publications, Inc. Available at: https://doi.org/10.4135/9780857020093

Senge, P. (1990) *The Fifth Discipline: The Art and Practice of the Learning Organization*, New York: Doubleday.

Sengupta, B. and Jantzen, R. (2018) 'Does broken windows policing reduce felony crime?', *International Journal of Applied Economics*, 15(1), 24–41.

Sharot, T. (2017) *The Influential Mind: What the Brain Reveals About Our Power to Change Others*, New York: Henry Holt & Company.

Sherman, L. (1998) *Evidence-Based Policing: Ideas in American Policing*, Washington, DC: National Police Foundation.

Sherman, L. (2013) 'The rise of evidence-based policing: Targeting, testing, and tracking', *Crime and Justice*, 42(1): 377–451.

Sherman, L. (2015) 'A tipping point for "totally evidenced policing": Ten ideas for building an evidence-based police agency', *International Criminal Justice Review*, 25(1): 11–29.

Sherman, L. (2015) *Evidence-Based Policing in 100 discoveries*, Somersham: Cambridge Centre for Evidence-Based Policing (Cambridge-ebp.net).

Sherman, L. and Eck, J. (2002) 'Policing for Crime Prevention', in L. Sherman, D. Farrington, B. Welsh, and D. MacKenzie (eds) *Evidence Based Crime Prevention*, Abingdon: Routledge, 295–329.

Sherman, L. and Murray, A. (2015) 'Evidence-based policing: From academics to professionals', *International Criminal Justice Review*, 25(1): 7–10.

Sherman, L. and Weisburd, D. (1995) 'General deterrent effects of police patrol in crime "hot spots": A randomized, controlled trial', *Justice Quarterly*, 12(4): 625–48.

Sherman, L., MacKenzie, D., Farrington, D., and Welsh, B. (eds) (2002) *Evidence Based Crime Prevention*, Abingdon: Routledge.

Silverman, D. (2001) *Interpreting Qualitative Data: Methods for Analysing Talk, Text and Interaction* (2nd edn), London, Thousand Oaks, CA and New Delhi: Sage.

Sinek, S. (2009) *Start with Why: How Great Leaders Inspire Everyone to Take Action*, New York: Portfolio.

Skogan, W. (2019) 'Advocate: Community Policing', in D. Weisburd and A. Braga (eds) *Police Innovation: Contrasting Perspectives* (2nd edn), Cambridge: Cambridge University Press, 27–44.

Skogan, W. and Frydl, K. (eds) (2004) *Fairness and Effectiveness in Policing: The Evidence*, Washington, DC: National Academies Press.

Skolnick, J. (1966) *Justice Without Trial: Law Enforcement in Democratic Society*, New York: Macmillan.

Skubak Tillyer, M., Engel, R., and Lovins, B. (2012) 'Beyond Boston: Applying theory to understand and address sustainability issues in focused deterrence initiatives for violence reduction', *Crime & Delinquency*, 58(6): 973–97.

Slothower, M., Neyroud, P., and Sherman, L. (2015) 'Tracking quality of police actions in a victim contact program: A case study of training, tracking, and feedback (TTF) in evidence-based policing', *International Criminal Justice Review*, 25(1): 98–116.

Smith, J., Santos, R., and Santos, R. (2018) 'Evidence-based policing and the stratified integration of crime analysis in police agencies: National survey results', *Policing: A Journal of Policy and Practice*, 12(3): 303–15.

Spector, B. (2011) *Implementing Organizational Change: Theory into Practice*, Upper Saddle River, NJ: Prentice Hall.

SPI (Strategies for Policing Innovation) (2020, November) Available at: www.strategiesforpolicinginnovation.com/tta/webinars

Stenson, K. and Edwards, A. (2001) 'Rethinking Crime Control in Advanced Liberal Government: "The Third Way" and the Return to the Local', in K. Stenson and R. Sullivan (eds) *Crime, Risk and Justice: The Politics of Crime Control in Liberal Democracies*, Cullompton: Willan, 68–86.

Strang, H., Sherman, L., Ariel, B., Chilton, S., et al (2017) 'Reducing the harm of intimate partner violence: Randomized controlled trial of the Hampshire Constabulary CARA experiment', *Cambridge Journal of Evidence-Based Policing*, 1, 160–173. Available at: https://doi.org/10.1007/s41887-017-0007-x

Stuart, F. (2020) *Ballad of the Bullet: Gangs, Drill Music and the Power of Online Infamy*, Princeton, NJ: Princeton University Press.

Sunshine, J. and Tyler, T. (2003) 'The role of procedural justice for legitimacy in shaping public support for policing', *Law and Society Review*, 37(3): 513–48.

Syed, M. (2015) *Black Box Thinking: The Surprising Truth about Success*, London: John Murray.

Sytsma, V. and Piza, E. (2018) 'Quality over quantity: Assessing the impact of frequent public interaction compared to problem-solving activities on police officer job satisfaction', *Policing: A Journal of Policy and Practice*, 14(2): 526–41. Available at: https://academic.oup.com/policing/advance-article-abstract/doi/10.1093/police.pay033/5037739

Taniguchi, T. and Bueermann, J. (2012) 'The embedded criminologist', Paper presented at the Ideas in American Policing Series, National Police Foundation, Washington, DC. Available at: http://ttaniguchi.net/wp-content/uploads/2014/08/Taniguchi-Bueermann-2012-Embedded-Criminologist.pdf

Taylor, B., Kowalyk, A., and Boba, R. (2007) 'The integration of crime analysis into law enforcement agencies: An exploratory study into the perceptions of crime analysts', *Police Quarterly*, 10(2), 154–69. doi:10.1177/1098611107299393

Telep, C.W. (2017) 'Police officer receptivity to research and evidence-based policing: Examining variability within and across agencies', *Crime & Delinquency*, 63(8): 976–99.

Telep, C.W. and Lum, C. (2014) 'The receptivity of officers to empirical research and evidence-based policing: An examination of survey data from three agencies', *Policing Quarterly*, 17(4): 359–84.

Telep, C.W. and Somers, L. (2017) 'Examining police officer definitions of evidence-based policing: Are we speaking the same language?', *Policing & Society*, 29(2): 171–87. doi:10.108 0/10439463.2017.1373775

Telep, C.W., Mitchell, R.J., and Weisburd, D. (2014) 'How much time should the police spend at crime hot spots? Answers from a police agency directed randomized field trial in Sacramento, California', *Justice Quarterly*, 31(5), 905–933. Available at: http://dx.doi.org/10.1080/07418825.2012.710645

Tett, G. (2016) *The Silo Effect: The Peril of Expertise and the Promise of Breaking Down Barriers*, New York: Simon & Schuster.

Thompson, V. (1965) 'Bureaucracy and innovation', *Administrative Science Quarterly*, 10(1), 1–20. doi:10.2307/2391646

Townsley, M., Homel, R., and Chaseling, J. (2000) 'Repeat burglary victimisation: Spatial and temporal patterns', *Australian and New Zealand Journal of Criminology*, 33(1): 37–63.

Tyler, T., Schulhofer, S., and Huq, A.Z. (2010) 'Legitimacy and deterrence effects in counterterrorism policing: A study of Muslim Americans', *Law & Society Review*, 44(2): 365–402.

Uman, L. (2011) 'Systematic reviews and meta-analysis', *Canadian Academy of Child and Adolescent Psychiatry*, 20(1): 57–9.

Vito, G., Walsh, W., and Kunselman, J. (2005) 'CompStat: The manager's perspective', *International Journal of Police Science and Management*, 7(3): 187–96.

Wallace, D., White, M.D., Gaub, J., and Todak, N. (2018) 'Body-worn cameras as a potential source of de-policing: Testing for camera-induced passivity', *Criminology*, 56(3): 481–509.

Weisburd, D. and Britt, C. (2014) *Statistics in Criminal Justice* (4th edn), New York: Springer.

Weisburd, D. and Eck, J.E. (2004) 'What can the police do to reduce crime, disorder, and fear?', *The Annals of the American Academy of Political and Social Science*, 593, 42–65.

Weisburd, D. and Majmundar, M. (2018) *Proactive Policing: Effects on Crime and Communities*, Washington, DC: The National Academies Press.

Weisburd, D. and Neyroud, P. (2011) 'Police science: Toward a new paradigm', *New Perspectives in Policing*, January. Available at: www.ncjrs.gov/pdffiles1/nij/228922.pdf

Weisburd, D., Telep, C.W., Hinkle, J.C., and Eck, J.E. (2010) 'Is problem-oriented policing effective in reducing crime and disorder? Findings from a Campbell systematic review', *Criminology and Public Policy*, 9, 139–72.

West, S. and O'Neal, K.K. (2004) 'Project DARE outcome effectiveness revisited', *American Journal of Public Health*, 94(6): 1027–29.

White, P. (2017) *Developing Research Questions* (2nd edn), Basingstoke: Palgrave Macmillan.

White, M. and Pooley, M. (2018) 'Testing the impact of de-escalation training of officer behavior: The Tempe, Arizona SPI Department', Paper presented to The Tempe, AZ Police Department.

Wieslander, M. (2018) 'Learning the (hidden) silence policy within the police', *Studies in Continuing Education*. doi:10.1080/0158037X.2018.1497592.

Williams, S. and Coupe, T. (2017) 'Frequency vs length of hot spots patrols: A randomised controlled trial', *Cambridge Journal of Evidence Based Policing*, 1(1): 1–5.

Willis, J. and Mastrofski, S.D. (2018) 'Improving policing by integrating craft and science: What can patrol officers teach us about good police work?', *Policing & Society*, 28(1): 27–44.

Willis, J., Mastrofski, S.D., and Weisburd, D. (2007) 'Making sense of CompStat: A theory-based analysis of organizational change in three police departments', *Law and Society Review*, 41: 147–88.

Wilson, J.Q. and Kelling, G.L. (1982) 'Broken windows: The police and neighborhood safety', *The Atlantic Monthly*, 211, 29–38.

Wolfe, S., Rojek, J., McLean, K., and Alpert, G. (2020) 'Social interaction training to reduce police use of Force', *The ANNALS of the American Academy of Political and Social Science*, 687(1): 124–45.

Wood, J. and Shearing, C. (2007) *Imagining Security*, New York: Routledge.

Wyllie, D. and Dudley, J. (2019) *Policing Matters*, Podcast, Police 1. Available at: www.police1.com/podcast/

Yokum, D., Ravishankar, A., and Coppock, A. (2019) 'A randomized control trial evaluating the effects of body-worn cameras', *PNAS: Proceedings of the National Academy of Sciences of the United States of America*, 116(21): 10329–32.

Zimring, F.E. (2013) *The City that Became Safe: New York's Lessons for Urban Crime and Its Control*, New York: Oxford University Press.

Index

References to figures and tables are in *italics*

Index

219